JUL 2 7 2022

YOU ARE A
CHAMPION

MARCUS RASHFORD

YOU ARE A CHAMPION

HOW TO BE THE BEST YOU CAN BE

written with Carl Anka

with contributions from Katie Warriner

FEIWEL AND FRIENDS

NEW YORK

TO EVERY YOUNG PERSON WHO IS TRYING
TO FIND THEIR WAY.

TO MY MUM, FOR HELPING ME TO BELIEVE
THAT DREAMS CAN COME TRUE.

A Feiwel and Friends Book
An imprint of Macmillan Publishing Group, LLC
120 Broadway, New York, NY 10271 • mackids.com

Our books may be purchased in bulk for promotional, educational, or business use.
Please contact your local bookseller or the Macmillan Corporate and Premium Sales
Department at (800) 221-7945 ext. 5442 or by email at
MacmillanSpecialMarkets@macmillan.com.

Library of Congress Control Number: 2022901698

First US edition, 2022
Book design by Janene Spencer and Veronica Mang
Feiwel and Friends logo designed by Filomena Tuosto
Printed in the United States of America by
Lakeside Book Company, Harrisonburg, Virginia

ISBN 978-1-250-85916-7 (hardcover)
1   3   5   7   9   10   8   6   4   2

Credits
Quote on page 67 used with the kind permission of Authentic Brands Group.
Graphics on pages 25, 102, 105 © www.moonshotseries.co.uk.
Image on page 157 © Liz Fosslien.

CONTENTS

I WANT TO START THIS BOOK BY TELLING YOU A STORY.

On July 11, 2021, England faced Italy in the final of UEFA Euro 2020.

(I know, it's confusing to have a tournament called Euro 2020 in the summer of 2021, but COVID-19 caused a delay on a lot of things!)

We love soccer in England. It's the most popular sport in the country. Everyone learns how to play it at school, and most weekends, thousands and thousands of people go to stadiums around the country to watch their favorite soccer team play. So England playing in a European final was a BIG deal!

It was the first time we had made it to the final of an international tournament since the World Cup in 1966. Soccer fans had waited fifty-five years for this moment, and to make things even better, the final was being held in Wembley Stadium in London. Just like in 1966, England was playing in a final at home. Everyone across the country was really excited.

All summer long, fans in England were singing funny, lighthearted songs about how soccer was going to come "home," back to England, the country that helped invent the sport. There were loads of newspaper articles about the England players and the manager, and people even joked that it would be a national holiday the day after if England won. That final really felt like it was going to be a special moment for everyone. England was going to win UEFA Euro 2020 and bring the trophy home. Fans thought we were going to be European Champions.

Unfortunately, that didn't happen.

England scored an early goal, but we had some trouble after that—Italy was really good. I watched nearly all of that match from the substitute bench, seeing how Italy was getting more of the ball and controlling the pace of the game, until they eventually got a goal back, making the score 1–1. The game went into extra time, and in the last moments of the match, the England manager, Gareth Southgate, put me on for the penalty shootout.

A penalty shootout is a special way to decide a winner if a soccer match ends in a draw. It doesn't happen in all soccer matches, but in big cup competitions, if no winner can be decided at the end of normal time (90 minutes) and extra time (an extra 30 minutes), then a penalty shootout is used to decide a winner.

In my opinion, a penalty shootout is soccer in its simplest form. It's one-on-one soccer, one attacker vs. one goalkeeper, where the attacker's task is to score a goal and the goalkeeper must stop that from happening. Each team nominates five attackers to take a penalty, and in the end, the team that scores the most penalties wins the whole game.

Five kicks of a ball to win a game of soccer. It sounds simple. Most weeks when I am playing for England or Manchester United, we will have a small session at the end of training where we all take penalties, and nearly everyone scores. But when it comes to a big game, where you have to take a penalty in front of thousands of soccer fans, with millions more watching at home? It's often less about skill and more about the fine margins. Penalty shootouts can be nerve-racking, one of the hardest things to do as a professional soccer player, and some of the best players in the world have missed penalties in shootouts. England has a poor record with shootouts (I'll tell you more about that later), and most of the time, soccer teams will go out of their way to make sure a game is finished so they can avoid one.

I was nominated to take the third penalty for England against Italy. By the time I stepped up to take my shot, Italy had scored two of their three attempts, while England had scored their first two. My kick would have taken England 3–2 up in the shootout and given us a big advantage for the remaining penalties.

I went up to take my penalty with nearly 60,000 England fans cheering me on. The Italian goalkeeper, a man called Gianluigi Donnarumma, is one of the biggest goalkeepers in the world of soccer, standing six feet, four inches tall. At my level of soccer, the goal is eight feet tall and eight yards wide, so I want you to imagine this BIG man filling up most of the space in this BIG goal, making it hard to score.

When I took my penalty, I took a stuttering run up, where I paused a little bit on my way to kick the ball in an attempt to make Donnarumma move early and make the penalty easier. By the time I got to the ball to take my shot, I had managed to get Donnarumma to guess the wrong way . . . but my shot missed the goal by an inch, hitting the post and going wide.

It was the biggest game of my international soccer career. The biggest game for the England team and fans in fifty-five years. And in one of the most important moments, I missed a chance to give us a lead. In the end, England lost that final 3—2 to Italy.

I felt terrible after that game. July 11, 2021, isn't one of my favorite days. It's not a date on the calendar I'll be looking for in the future.

The day after that final, some people said some pretty hurtful things about myself, my manager, and some of my teammates who also missed penalties. It was tough. As a professional athlete, people often talk about what you do in the Big Moments, whether you won or lost the game and what you did to help, or not help, your team. Back in 2019, I played in a game for Manchester United against Paris Saint-Germain in the UEFA Champions League, where I was asked to take a penalty in the final minutes. It was this huge moment, and I had to score for Manchester United to get through to the next round. That time, I managed to score, and it felt great. But in the days after missing a penalty for England and losing the UEFA Euro 2020 final, I didn't feel great. There is a painting of my face in a town in Manchester where I grew up, and someone was so angry that I didn't score my penalty that they vandalized it. That really hurt me. Sometimes you can kick the ball right and you're a hero. Other times you miss and people call you a zero.

BUT THEN SOMETHING AMAZING HAPPENED.

In the days following the final, people from all over the UK traveled to the painting and left messages of support for me and my teammates.

Now, you might be wondering why I've started a book called *You Are a Champion* with a story about *losing* a game for a championship. But I'm telling you this story to show you that there's more than one way to win.

IN SPORTS. IN LIFE. IN EVERYTHING.

England had lost a final, but in the days following, I won something else: the knowledge that people from all over the country were rooting for the

England team, including myself. That in the face of abuse, people were standing alongside one another to block out the negative noise. They were protecting me.

I know it's not the same, and I know a part of me will always think about that penalty and the final we never won. But on that day—July 11, 2021—and in the days after, I learned that there can be more than one way of winning. You might not always get a trophy or the medal you wanted, but if you go out there with your head held high and try your best, you've already won.

MY NAME IS MARCUS RASHFORD,
AND I WANT YOU TO KNOW THAT
YOU ARE A CHAMPION.

This book is my attempt to pass on some of the lessons I've picked up along my life's journey. Things that have helped me through tough times and things that have helped me find and celebrate the good. I want you to know that there are people out there who believe in you, and who understand you are at the start of your life's journey—a journey that can be the most incredible thing. My journey has taken me to some really interesting places, and something I've always tried to remember is that there are no limits to what is possible in this life. I know it isn't always the smoothest, and sometimes you might get stuck and need help, but you are capable of amazing things.

Within you right now is the most incredible potential to go out there and chase your dreams, to be a champion in almost anything you put your mind to, because there are so many different ways you can be one!

You can be a champion in a competition and come out number one, but you can also still be a champion in the things you enjoy even if you don't win prizes for them. I want to help you develop skills for the challenges ahead so you can be a champion at life.

You can be a champion for another person, and try your best to support them in what they do. I hope you'll learn that there are people around you who are championing you right now, and that you can even be a champion for the people who are close to you, too.

You can be a champion for a cause. Back in England, I've been involved in a few anti-food-poverty campaigns, trying to get food to people who need it most, because that's a cause very close to my heart. You might decide you want to be a champion for something you believe in, and I'd like to show you how to do that.

And no matter what happens in your life, the most amazing way that you can be a champion is by being your OWN champion. Trust me, when you believe in yourself, incredible things can happen.

I want you to think of this book as a key that unlocks new doors in your mind, and I hope that in reading this you find something useful for all the years ahead. I hope that by the time you get to the last page you'll have found some new ways of thinking that will help you. Everyone is different, everyone has their own journey, but everyone, in their own special way, is a champion.

SO LET'S FIND OUT ALL THE WAYS THAT YOU ARE A CHAMPION.

Turn that page and let's get to work.

Together.

M.R.

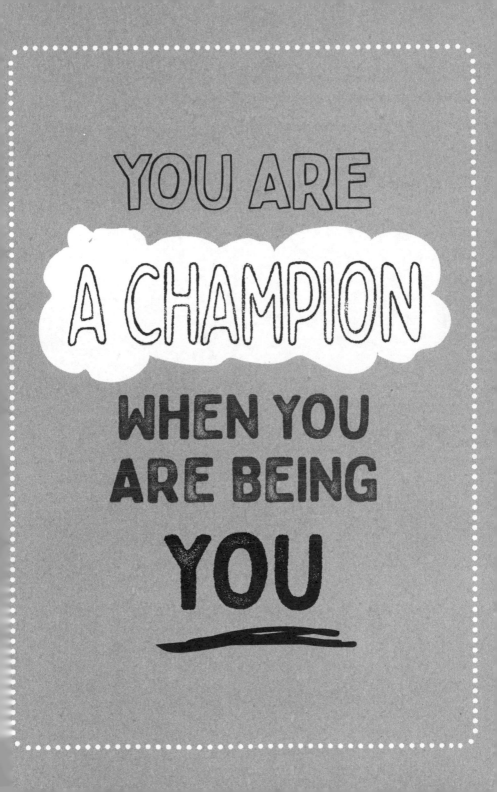

1

THERE ARE PROBABLY A LOT OF THINGS YOU KNOW ABOUT ME ALREADY. I play as a forward for Manchester United and England, which means I have to try my best to create or score goals whenever possible. I'm right-footed, although I'm working on getting better on my left. I'm the youngest of five siblings—I have two older brothers, Dwaine and Dane, and two sisters, Chantelle and Claire—and my mum's name is Melanie. I love them all a lot. Family is really important to me, and I like to help people, too—that's one reason why I work hard on things I'm passionate about, both on and off the field.

There are also lots of things you might not know about me. I don't have a middle name, but one of the first nicknames I ever had was "Shot," because once I was playing in goal, and I took a shot right in the face, then I sprang back up like it was nothing. (It ended up being an epic save!)

When I was a kid, I wasn't the best swimmer and I was also a little scared of heights, but I loved strawberry cream cookies. My favorite Ninja Turtle was Donatello, although I wasn't great at science in school like he was—I was better at math. I grew up by Button Lane in Wythenshawe, South Manchester, and I used to sleep on the top bunk in a bedroom I shared with my brother Dane. We had a little TV on top of this set of cupboards, but it didn't work all the time, and sometimes you'd have to give it a bang when the picture was getting fuzzy.

When I was growing up, my days used to follow a pretty standard pattern: I'd wake up, eat two Weetabix for breakfast (covered in sugar), I'd go to school, do the lessons, play soccer at break time and lunch-time, then at the end of the day I'd go home. On the way, I'd always look for a rock, or drink can, or anything I could pretend was a ball so I could kick it home. Soccer has always been on my brain that way. Some days I would go to the park after school, but if I couldn't do that, then I'd be playing soccer in my garden, working on my skills, or hanging out with my friends.

That was me up until about the age of 11, which was when I moved into digs (a kind of house young players move to when they join a soccer academy) to be closer to Manchester United. And a lot of that is still me now that I'm an adult—I'm better with heights, but I still like strawberry cream cookies, and I love cereal (especially Coco Pops).

On top of that, there's also a bunch of new things that I'm beginning to enjoy: I like music a lot more now, and I've been trying to learn how to play the guitar and the piano (although I find the guitar way easier). I'm also trying to learn some languages—I think Spanish is very cool. (Or, *muy guay*, as they say!)

All of this makes up the person I used to be, the person I am now, and the person I'm working to be in the future. A lot of it has stayed the same since I was a kid, but a lot of it has changed, too.

AND NO MATTER WHAT HAS HAPPENED IN MY LIFE, NO MATTER WHAT I'M WORKING TOWARD, I'M ALWAYS MARCUS. 100% MARCUS RASHFORD. BECAUSE THAT'S THE ONLY PERSON I CAN BE.

6

And I want you to be **you**.

>>> YOU <<<

THE PERSON
READING THIS.

I want you to be you,
and I want you to be the
best version of you
that you can be.

Don't get me wrong, I know that can be really tough sometimes.
*IT'S SO EASY TO LOOK AT OTHER PEOPLE AND WISH
YOU HAD WHAT THEY HAD, OR EVEN WISH YOU WERE
SOMEONE ELSE ENTIRELY.* We've all been there. You might look at
me and think, "Why would Marcus Rashford ever want to be someone
else?!" But trust me, I've been there.

WHEN I WAS GROWING UP, THERE WERE PLENTY OF TIMES WHEN THINGS WEREN'T GOING MY WAY AND I WISHED LIFE COULD BE DIFFERENT FOR ME.

I used to spend a lot of time around my brother Dane and his friends—this was when I was about 4 or 5, so they would have been around 9 or 10. They would go to Hollyhedge Park, this big park near where we lived, to play soccer all the time. And I wanted to join in

more

than

ANYTHING.

I LOVE SOCCER.

It might be a bit silly to say, considering I play for Manchester United, but

FOR AS LONG AS I CAN REMEMBER, ALL I'VE WANTED TO DO IS PLAY. It doesn't matter what position I'm playing in, what the weather's like, or who the opponent is, if you give me a chance to play, that's what I'm going to do.

But when I was following around my brother and his friends, there were often times I wasn't allowed to play, and that used to really wind me up—

SOMETIMES I WASN'T ALLOWED BECAUSE MY BROTHER WAS WITH SOME OLDER BOYS WHO WERE A BIT ROUGH AND HE DIDN'T WANT ME TO GET HURT, AND OTHER TIMES I WASN'T ALLOWED BECAUSE SOME OF THE KIDS WERE WEARING SOCCER CLEATS.

I didn't have any of my own, and it can be pretty painful if someone steps on you wearing soccer cleats, especially when you're not wearing them. I'm an adult now, and it still hurts when someone tackles me in cleats!

But when I was a kid, I didn't care about that stuff. Not being allowed to play didn't feel great, and it made me feel really frustrated. I spent a lot of time on the sidelines, watching Dane play with his friends, wishing that I'd get a chance to join in.

There are going to be times in your life when you're not going to be able to do the things you want to. This might make you feel trapped, and that might hurt for you. It's never a great feeling being on the sidelines and watching other people do the things you really want to do in life, and when you feel stuck, your mind might start to wander and you'll think about how things could be different. How situations could be different. Sometimes you might start to think about the ways YOU could be different.

I know it can be easy to compare ourselves to other people, but it's important to remember that you can only be the best version of yourself that you can be. *YOU ARE A CHAMPION AT BEING YOU.* Whenever I'm feeling frustrated with the way things are going, this is what I always come back to:

YOU ARE ONLY IN COMPETITION WITH YOURSELF, SO STOP COMPARING YOURSELF TO OTHER PEOPLE.

WISHING THINGS WERE DIFFERENT WON'T CHANGE ANYTHING, AND THAT TIME YOU SPEND WISHING IS TIME YOU COULD HAVE SPENT CHANGING WHAT IS ACTUALLY IN YOUR CONTROL. You're not in competition with anyone else, so you only need to work on being the best version of yourself that you can be.

All that time I spent on the edge of Hollyhedge Park, even though I was thinking about being someone else, no matter what happened, I couldn't be. I couldn't be my brother with his soccer cleats. I couldn't be a bigger boy with different skills. I couldn't play soccer as much as I wanted. All of that was out of my control. I could only be Marcus, the small skinny kid from around the corner who loves soccer but who sometimes couldn't play.

So in the end, I decided to figure out what **WAS** in my control and to change what I could. Instead of staring at my brother and his friends from the sidelines, just wishing I could play, I started doing kick-ups, working on my soccer skills, and doing tricks with a little size 1 ball. **I DECIDED TO GET USED TO BEING MARCUS AND WORKED ON BEING THE BEST VERSION OF MARCUS I COULD BE WHILE I WAITED FOR ANOTHER TIME I COULD PLAY.** And all that time I spent on the sidelines working on my soccer skills ended up being really useful for me now in my career!

ONE OF THE THINGS I LIKE MOST ABOUT SOCCER IS THAT ANYONE, OF ANY SIZE OR ANY WEIGHT, CAN MAKE IT AS A PROFESSIONAL SOCCER PLAYER IF THEY HAVE THE SKILL AND ARE WILLING TO WORK HARD.

For me growing up, it wasn't about wanting to be someone else so I could play soccer, but working with what I had. There are people playing soccer who might be short but have brilliant agility, so they can turn really fast, which taller people can have problems with. Or there are tall players who are good in the air and do things other players can't. There's no one set way to be an amazing soccer player. I definitely had heroes growing up—Wayne Rooney, Cristiano Ronaldo, and Tim Howard to name a few!—and I wanted to be **like** these other players when I was a kid. But I knew that I could never be **exactly** like them, and if I'd tried, I wouldn't have ended up being the Marcus Rashford you know today. *I HAD TO WORK WITH WHAT LIFE GAVE ME.*

THERE ARE GOING TO BE LOADS OF THINGS THAT YOU'LL WANT TO DO IN LIFE—SOME OF THEM YOU'RE GOING TO BE GREAT AT, SOME OF THEM YOU MIGHT BE LESS GOOD AT. (I'm still not the best swimmer, but I'm working on it!) There are also loads of brilliant things that will happen that you can't possibly predict—there's so much you haven't tried yet that you're going to be amazing at, but you won't find that out until the time comes. There are always new things to learn—your brain is like a sponge that's

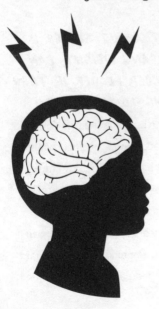

constantly picking information up from the world around you!—but a good starting place for a lot of life's adventures is learning who you are, learning to be comfortable with that, then deciding what you want to do. When you are true to yourself, the progress you make lasts a lot longer because you're making good decisions that you can repeat again and again.

THERE ARE OVER SEVEN BILLION PEOPLE ON PLANET EARTH.

THAT'S 7,000,000,000 PEOPLE WITH THEIR OWN LIKES, DISLIKES, FAVORITE FOODS, COLORS, FILMS, AND BOOKS ALL GOING ABOUT THEIR LIVES, TRYING TO DO THEIR BEST. THERE ARE A LOT OF PEOPLE IN THIS WORLD WHO WILL BE SIMILAR TO YOU, BUT NO ONE OUT THERE IS GOING TO BE <u>EXACTLY</u> LIKE YOU.

TAKE A MOMENT TO LOOK AT YOUR HANDS RIGHT NOW; NO ONE WHO WOKE UP TODAY HAS THE SAME FINGERPRINTS THAT YOU HAVE.

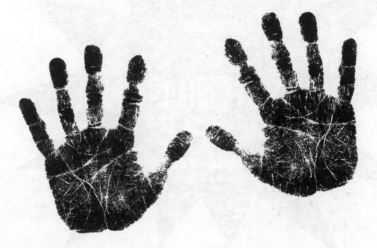

Stick your tongue out. I know it sounds silly, but do it. Blow a big raspberry with it. No one who is going to bed tonight has the same tongue as you. Seriously, tongues are just as unique as fingerprints!

Did blowing a raspberry just now make you smile? Did it make you laugh? No one out there is going to have the exact same laugh as you, either, or laugh at the exact same things that you find funny.

And while all sorts of things might happen that will make you feel differently about your life—your hair color or your favorite film might change, or you might decide one day that the food you used to hate actually tastes really good (it took me a long time to enjoy fish, but traveling has opened my eyes to different foods!)—the person you wake up as is going to have a lot in common with the person you go to bed as.

Even when big things change, that still won't shift who you are. You can move house, or your name might change, but you're still going to be **YOU** every single day.

It can be a little scary when you think about it, but I think it can be a good scary. There are going to be days when you might wish you were someone else, or you'll wish you were a different version of yourself, or you might want to be "normal" or feel like you fit in better. *IT CAN BE REALLY SCARY BEING YOU SOMETIMES BECAUSE NO ONE HAS EVER DONE IT BEFORE. BUT THAT'S OKAY!* While people might be similar to you, no one is ever going to be as good at being you as you are—even if they wanted to, and put all their money and talent and time into trying.

That's how unique every single person is. And that's why we shouldn't spend so much time worrying and comparing ourselves to other people. Instead *WE SHOULD BE THINKING ABOUT ALL THE AMAZING THINGS WE CAN DO.*

YOU CAN ONLY
EVER BE

YOU

IN THIS LIFE,
SO WHY DON'T YOU
SPEND THIS TIME
TRYING TO BECOME
THE BEST EVER
VERSION OF YOU
THAT YOU CAN BE?

There are seven billion people in this world, and no one is going to have the same fingerprints and hands as you. So rather than use your hands to point at other people and think, "I want what they have!" you can point to yourself and go, "I am completely unique and special, and if I work hard and stay true to myself, I can do amazing things."

YOU ARE AT YOUR MOST
POWERFUL
WHEN YOU ARE
BEING YOU

When you start being you, as proudly as you can be, so many things are possible. When you work on figuring out who you are, what you are good at, and where you can improve, that version of you gets **stronger and stronger and stronger and stronger.**

And remember that there is so much more to you than what you do. I'm Marcus and I play soccer, but when the full-time whistle blows, I don't stop being me.

You're already a champion at being yourself, and I want to help you figure out how to be the best champion of yourself you can possibly be. When you start by championing yourself, you find it easier to become a champion at loads of other things.

That's my aim. I never try to compete with anybody else. If you wake up and try to be the best version of yourself you can be, then no matter what happens to you that day, you can't go to bed as a failure. *IF YOU GIVE YOUR BEST AT DOING THE THING YOU ARE BEST AT—BEING YOU—THEN YOU'VE DONE SOMETHING NO ONE ELSE IN THE WORLD CAN DO.*

1. FIND THE CHAMPION IN YOU

HOPEFULLY THIS CHAPTER HAS HELPED YOU SEE
THAT YOU ARE A COMPLETE ONE-OFF—YOU ARE
A CHAMPION WHEN YOU ARE BEING YOU. SO LET'S
GET TO KNOW YOU BETTER.

Have a look at the following questions. You could think about your
answers in your head, write them down in a notebook, or, better still,
chat about them with a friend or family member:

- What makes you laugh?
- What is your favorite food?
- What have you tried hard at in your life so far?
- Who do you care about?
- What are you proud of?
- What are you good at?
- What would you like to get better at?
- What are you thankful for?

2. ENJOY COMPETING WITH YOURSELF

You are only in competition with yourself, so stop comparing yourself to other people. Imagine that the you of today is meeting the you of this time two years ago. What would they say to each other? Have a think about the following:

- What can the you of today do that the you of last year couldn't?

- What are you better at today? Any new skills? New things you've learned about? New people you've met? Remember that your brain today is stronger than it was two years ago—what can it do now that it couldn't do before?

- What has helped you get better? Have you worked hard? Have people helped you?

If you work hard and focus on being the best you can be, you can make your best better every day. It might not feel like you are making progress, but if you keep working, lots of small wins each day add up to big wins over time!

3. FOCUS ON WHAT YOU CAN CONTROL

TO BE THE BEST YOU CAN BE, I NEED YOU TO FOCUS ON WHAT YOU CAN CONTROL. IT'S NORMAL FOR OUR MINDS TO WANDER, BUT REMEMBER THAT YOU ARE THE BOSS. When you have something you want to get better at, get a piece of paper and draw a big circle. Write down everything that you can control on the inside of the circle, and everything that you can't control on the outside of the circle. Try to have at least three things on the inside, and three things on the outside. Here is an example for when I had to give a talk at school that I was nervous about:

HOW MUCH I
PREPARE FOR IT

TRYING MY BEST

MY ATTITUDE

OTHER PEOPLE'S
ATTENTION SPAN

WHAT MARK I GET

HOW OTHER PEOPLE
THINK OF ME

When I focused on the things outside the circle, I felt worried and less confident because I couldn't control those things. When I focused on the things inside the circle, I felt positive and more confident. This is a skill you can get better at by practicing it lots. I know it will help you be a champion at being you.

DARE TO DREAM

2

Five years ago, I made my debut for Manchester United. It went pretty well—I scored two goals in an important Europa League game to help my team win. In doing so, *I BECAME THE YOUNGEST EVER GOALSCORER FOR MY CLUB IN A EUROPEAN COMPETITION.*

Five years before that, I was 13 years old, trying to figure out how to do some of the soccer skills in a training book I'd been given by a coach in United's academy. That went . . . good at times, but other times I got stuck, or a bit frustrated, or confused about how to pull off certain tricks. (And I'll tell you a bit more about that later.)

Five years before that, I was 8 years old, just starting out on this soccer journey. I didn't have much when I was growing up, so I had no idea my life could ever end up like this. Back then I didn't even know that being a soccer player could be your real job! *I WAS JUST A KID WHO LOVED SOCCER, AND I WANTED TO BE THE BEST I COULD BE AT IT.*

It's hard to know what is possible until you start. You have to be able to dream big and be prepared to work toward your dreams.

I'm 23 now and I've achieved a lot, but it didn't come in one go.

BIG THINGS RARELY HAPPEN OVERNIGHT, AND GOOD THINGS RARELY HAPPEN AS IF BY MAGIC.

I scored on my debut, both for Manchester United and England. But the very first time I was selected for the senior team at United, I was a substitute against Watford and I was really nervous. It was the first time in my life that I'd had a chance to play senior team soccer, and I didn't know if I was ready to take to the field then and there.

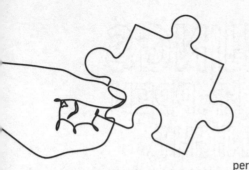

I like to think that a person's life is made up of all these different small puzzles, which come together to make one **HUGE** puzzle. When you start out, your personality and the world around you gives you different pieces to work with, and it's up to you how you want to make a picture with it. Your dreams can be as big as you want to make the puzzle.

AND JUST LIKE PUTTING TOGETHER A PUZZLE, THERE'LL BE SOME BITS THAT YOU'LL UNDERSTAND RIGHT AWAY AND ARE ABLE TO PUT INTO PLACE REALLY QUICKLY—you'll see parts of your life that will immediately make sense. But sometimes there will be bits that you won't be able to figure out until later; you'll have to spin them around a few times and think for a while until you can see where they fit.

YOU MIGHT GET SOME BITS
THAT FIT TOGETHER IN ONE
AREA, BUT YOU DON'T KNOW WHERE THEY FIT INTO
THE MUCH BIGGER PICTURE UNTIL A LITTLE FURTHER
DOWN THE LINE. SOME BITS OF A PUZZLE COME
EASILY. SOME BITS DON'T MAKE SENSE UNTIL THE
LAST MOMENT. AND THAT IS EXACTLY WHAT LIFE
CAN BE LIKE.

When I was a kid, I had this dream of playing
soccer. As I got older, the picture in my head
became me playing soccer for Manchester
United. That's a **BIG** dream. So there had
to be loads of different pieces that went
into making it into a whole picture,
making it into a reality.

Some of those pieces happened really early in my life. When I was 4, bits of that dream were already fitting together; I liked soccer and I was playing every day (or at least kicking a ball, a can, or something else, pretending I was playing soccer). So that's already two pieces that went together and fitted into the bigger picture.

But there were also some parts I was trying to piece together that didn't fit into the bigger picture. Not yet. Remember how I used to watch on the sidelines in the park while my brother and his friends were playing soccer? The time when I would do kick-ups and other soccer skills, working on making myself better? I didn't know it then—as I was mainly frustrated that I couldn't actually play soccer—but that was me slowly putting together valuable pieces that would help get me closer to my dream.

I HAD A BIG DREAM, BUT IT TOOK LOADS OF LITTLE STEPS, LOADS OF SMALLER DREAMS, AND LOADS OF SMALL WAYS OF FIGURING MY LIFE OUT TO MAKE IT INTO A REALITY.

If you want to learn how to do something like play the guitar, you don't start off by learning a really complicated bit of music. You first have to get comfortable with holding a guitar, then learn how to strum, and then you learn a few chords. After that, you move on to pieces of music that only need two or three chords, then four chords, and then five and so on.

I think a lot of people go about figuring out their lives that way—step by step.

I WASN'T ALWAYS AS TALENTED AS THE MARCUS YOU SEE ON TV PLAYING FOR UNITED AND ENGLAND. When I first got on the ball and tried doing kick-ups, it didn't just work out magically. I didn't just manage to do 100 kick-ups the first time I tried. I could barely do two. So I had to find a way to get to where I wanted to be—my end goal was to be able to do loads of kick-ups, and I had to try to figure out a way to make that possible.

I SET MYSELF SMALLER GOALS TO BE ABLE TO ACHIEVE THE BIGGER GOAL, AND THEN I WORKED ON IT STEP BY STEP

When I first started doing kick-ups, I had to let the ball bounce in between each time it went off my foot. So my first step, my first puzzle piece, was to learn how to do kick-ups without the bounce. That took a lot of practice. A lot of kicking a ball around at home, in my garden, and at the park with my older brother.

PICTURE IT, ME TRYING TO JUGGLE A BALL ON MY FEET EVERY TIME I COULD. I MUST HAVE DRIVEN MY MUM AND BROTHERS UP THE WALL WITH THE NOISE!

Once I figured out how to do kick-ups while standing in place, without the bounce—which took a LOT of practice—I wanted to see if I could do them while I was moving, so I started walking around a bit while doing it.

Then I wanted to build up how far I could walk while doing kick-ups. There was a pavement outside our house that went in a semicircle, where I would set myself challenges for when I got home from school. I would try to walk around the semicircle once with the ball, but I let myself have one bounce in between each touch, as I knew it'd be harder to walk farther and do kick-ups. And then, when I could go around it once continuously doing kick-ups with one bounce in between, I set myself the challenge to go around it twice. And then three times. Eventually, I got to the stage where I could do kick-ups walking around the semicircle with a bounce in between as many times as I wanted. So then I set myself the challenge of walking around it, just once, without any bounces.

It took a while, and to do it I had to put loads of different things together, but eventually I learned how to do something I really wanted—to do kick-ups without letting the ball drop, even when I was walking. AND ALL THOSE SMALLER PIECES HELPED MAKE SOMETHING THAT IS REALLY IMPORTANT TO THE EVEN BIGGER PUZZLE I AM STILL TRYING TO MAKE NOW, WHICH IS TO BE THE BEST SOCCER PLAYER I CAN BE.

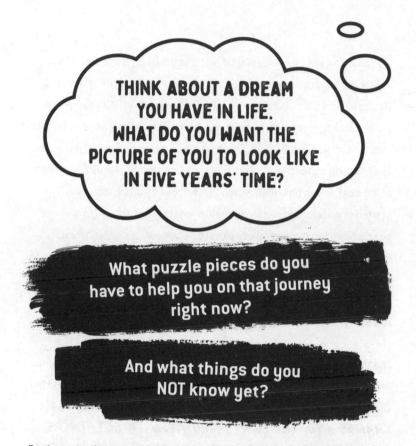

**THINK ABOUT A DREAM
YOU HAVE IN LIFE.
WHAT DO YOU WANT THE
PICTURE OF YOU TO LOOK LIKE
IN FIVE YEARS' TIME?**

**What puzzle pieces do you
have to help you on that journey
right now?**

**And what things do you
NOT know yet?**

Don't worry about not having all the pieces right now. Even though I knew I wanted to play soccer, I had no idea I was good enough to play for United until long after it happened. I joined Manchester United's academy in a place called Carrington when I was 9 years old. Carrington is like a school, but every subject there has to do with playing soccer, and every person who goes there is really talented at the sport. I was one of thirty 9-year-old boys, and every single one of them could do these amazing soccer skills. I didn't get there and think, "I've made it!" All I saw was a group of thirty great kids, just like me, and I started to think about where I could fit in. As time went on, I noticed less and less people in my group as the academy teachers and coaches decided to only focus on the best of the best. It was only then, when I was about 12 or 13, that I slowly started to understand more and realize what could happen to me—the puzzle pieces that made up my picture became a lot clearer. When I was 14, I played in a tournament called the England Victory Shield and I suddenly realized: *THIS IS HAPPENING. I'M GOOD ENOUGH TO BE A PROFESSIONAL SOCCER PLAYER ONE DAY IF I WORK HARD ENOUGH.*

The thing is, sometimes the picture you're working on won't make sense until after you've put all the pieces together. But what's important is that you never stop working toward your dreams. *THE PICTURE MAY CHANGE AND THE PARTS YOU NEED TO GET THERE MAY NEED TWEAKING, BUT YOU SHOULD NEVER STOP AIMING FOR WHAT YOU WANT.*

DREAM BIG

AS BIG AS YOU POSSIBLY CAN

When you **dream big**, you unlock all of this potential inside you. There's no limit on your imagination—your brain can come up with special effects and things way more amazing than any Hollywood film. When you start imagining amazing things happening for yourself, you unlock all these different paths inside of you.

I DIDN'T HAVE MUCH WHEN I WAS GROWING UP, AND LOOK AT WHERE I'VE ENDED UP. EVEN AT TIMES WHEN YOU MIGHT NOT HAVE MUCH, IT'S IMPORTANT TO KEEP DREAMING BIG. ONE OF THE BEST THINGS YOU CAN DO FOR YOURSELF IS IMAGINE A WORLD WHERE YOU CAN BE HAPPY. THE MORE YOU PICTURE THAT, THE EASIER IT BECOMES TO MAKE THAT PICTURE HAPPEN.

So try to paint the most amazing picture that you can for yourself—and then break it up into loads of small, achievable goals. Look at all of the different ways the world around you and the things you have in life now can work to make that big picture. Not everything is going to happen the way you want, or at the time you want, and things might change along the way, but you should never lose sight of what's important to you.

And remember to enjoy the journey—I'll admit there are certain times when I don't want to wake up early and go jogging so I can stay fit, but my journey in soccer has been a happy one because I **enjoy** playing soccer.

Try to make sure it's **YOUR** goal, too. Big dreams take a lot of hard work and can take a very long time to come together, so it's really important that you're working toward something that **YOU** want. When you start imagining having things that other people have, or comparing yourself to other people, it can be harder to figure out what you can do with the pieces you have.

It's when you're copying someone else, or trying to do something to impress someone else, that you might get knocked off your journey. When it's your dream, you're in control, and although you may get stuck, or frustrated, or want to quit at times, you'll always find a way to get back on track because you're the person who set the dream. Always remember that you're not in competition with anyone else but yourself.

THIS IS YOUR LIFE. YOUR DREAMS. YOUR BIG PUZZLE PICTURE. AND IT'S YOUR JOURNEY TRYING TO PUT THINGS TOGETHER.

YOU'RE GOING TO DO SO MANY AMAZING THINGS IN YOUR LIFE. There are going to be days when you learn new bits about yourself and end up getting those important pieces you need to get closer to your dreams. There are also going to be days when you learn something you don't even know you need yet—you might end up storing some valuable skill for years later, like me learning soccer skills on the sidelines rather than actually playing a game.

Think about how you're taking in all the information in this book—there was a point in your life when you wouldn't have been able to do that, but you slowly put loads of things together in your mind and now you can take in this information and use it to do other things in your life. One day you might decide you love reading, and end up taking on bigger, longer books. They might be in a different language, or you might decide that you prefer a different kind of book, or maybe even that books aren't for you right now, so you go off and develop a talent for something else. All of that is great— what's important is that you never stop thinking about the incredible things that you want to do.

AND ONCE YOU'VE DONE THAT,
THINK OF ALL THE WAYS YOU CAN
BREAK DOWN A PLAN THAT SEEMS
NEAR IMPOSSIBLE INTO SOMETHING...

SMALLER AND
ACHIEVABLE.

And remember that you are never alone when you are dreaming big. Whatever big picture you imagine for yourself, you should always try to place the people who care about you in there as well—no matter who they are. I didn't just dream of being a soccer player for Manchester United, I dreamed of being one because I wanted to look after my family and help provide for them. **MY FAMILY WAS ALWAYS IN MY BIG PICTURE, BECAUSE THEY GAVE ME LOADS OF THINGS TO HELP ME CHASE THE DREAM AND SUPPORTED ME ALONG THE WAY.**

It might sound silly to say **"SUCCESS DOESN'T HAPPEN OVERNIGHT"** and **"GOOD THINGS TAKE TIME"** when I had the debut I did, but you have to remember that I didn't appear out of nowhere at age 18 and start scoring goals for Manchester United. My journey started years before that, doing kick-ups in my back garden and watching YouTube clips of some of my favorite soccer players. Chasing your goal is hard, and achieving my soccer dream has taken hard work and dedication. Your dream isn't going to be handed to you on a plate— you need to keep working at it, and persevere even when things get tough. And when you get knocked down, you need to keep getting back up, time and time again.

Five years ago, loads of people were talking about me and my debut like it was some sort of fairy tale, but the most important thing that happened when I started playing for United wasn't that I scored, or that we won the game; it was when I came home and said to my family, **"MY PROMISE TO YOU GUYS IS THAT I'M NEVER GONNA CHANGE WHO I AM."**

I said, "The person that you've seen and known before the game today is going to be the same person for the rest of my career."

IT'S **REALLY IMPORTANT** TO DREAM AND TO SET GOALS, BUT IT'S ALSO IMPORTANT TO **NEVER LOSE SIGHT OF WHO YOU ARE AND WHAT'S IMPORTANT TO YOU.**

I can only be Marcus. And I can only dream big when I'm thinking like Marcus; otherwise I'll lose sight of my goals and be less effective. You need to chase your dreams with the right people around you and to never forget the things that have to happen for you to get what you want.

AND WHEN YOU THINK ABOUT THE LEVEL OF SUCCESS THAT YOU CAN REACH? DON'T EVER PUT A CAP ON IT. I DIDN'T. I STILL DON'T. I think that once you understand things about yourself, about the world, and what you want to do in it, then there is so much potential for what you can achieve.

I haven't even finished my puzzle, as new things are always coming into my life that change the picture. Life can surprise you with what it throws at you, so don't worry if your dream changes over time—you are going to come across so many opportunities on this journey, and things are always going to change.

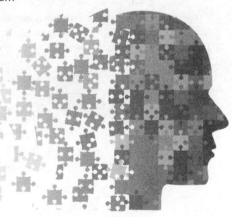

One big change for me happened when I was in my late teens: I looked at myself and decided I wanted to get better at reading books properly. *IT TOOK ME ABOUT TWO YEARS, BUT WITH PRACTICE, I FELT SOMETHING CHANGE IN ME. I BECAME MORE CONFIDENT IN MYSELF AND BETTER AT CHOOSING MY THOUGHTS AND WHAT I WANTED TO DO IN MY LIFE.*

When I was in primary school I didn't ever think I'd be a book person. Teachers used to give me books to help me get myself in order, but it was probably only when I went to high school, when I was about 11, that I found some books that helped me understand more about the world. I started enjoying them. Books helped me to think about what I wanted in the future, and I decided to write down those dreams—because for me, when you

write down your dream, you can hold it and feel it and give it life. Now I'm 23 and you're reading a book with my name on it, which seems really funny to me, but really cool too—I hope this book might help you dream big and start journeys of your own.

Sometimes big dreams can look difficult, and they might surprise you when they change, but you'll get there piece by piece. ***JUST MAKE SURE YOU NEVER STOP WORKING TOWARD THEM, WHATEVER THEY ARE.*** You'll learn loads about yourself and the world around you as you go.

And just like doing a puzzle, it's always easier when you have people you trust to help you put together the more difficult pieces along the way.

1. DARE TO DREAM

MAYBE YOU ALREADY HAVE A DREAM, MAYBE YOU ARE YET TO DISCOVER IT, OR MAYBE YOU HAVE LOTS OF DREAMS! WHEN I WAS A KID, I KNEW I WANTED TO PLAY SOCCER, BUT I DIDN'T KNOW I COULD PLAY FOR MANCHESTER UNITED. THIS IS WHY IT'S IMPORTANT TO DREAM BIG; YOU NEVER KNOW WHAT MIGHT BE POSSIBLE. I WANT YOU TO HAVE THE CHANCE TO DREAM ABOUT THE PERSON YOU'D LIKE TO BE AND ABOUT THE THINGS YOU'D LIKE TO DO. HAVE A THINK ABOUT THE FOLLOWING QUESTIONS:

- Imagine you are 21 years old. What sort of person do you want to be? What would you like your friends and family to say about you?

- Building on the person you'd like to be, what dreams do you have?

- If you knew you couldn't fail, what would your dream be?

- Close your eyes and imagine you've achieved your dream. How do you feel? What would be amazing about it?

2. FIND THE PIECES OF YOUR JIGSAW PUZZLE

Thinking about your dream can be really exciting, but it can also be a little scary. To help with this, we need to break it down into small pieces—you don't build a jigsaw puzzle in one go, you just put it together one piece at a time.

- How can you break your big dream into small dreams?
- What do you need to get better at?
- Who could help you?
- What can you learn from others?

3. FIND THE FIRST PIECE

My first piece to becoming a professional soccer player was practicing with a soccer ball every day. Now it's time to find yours. Write down or think about what the first steps are in achieving your dream. How can you turn that dream into a reality by taking that step? And if you'd like one more top tip—tell someone you care about what your dream is and what your first step is. This will help you focus on being the best you can be.

PRACTICE LIKE A CHAMPION

I'VE GOT A STORY FOR YOU ABOUT A BOOK.

When I was in the United academy, the coaches gave me a big booklet. It contained all these amazing soccer skills and taught me how to pull off even the hardest tricks.

The booklet broke each skill into a step-by-step process and showed you how to practice each one until it became second nature. It not only built your confidence, it also taught you the kind of dedication you'd need if you were going to make it as a professional soccer player.

The booklet had a whole load of skills that the coaches wanted every academy player to learn: five-yard dashes, how to pass and receive the ball between the lines, stepovers, kick-ups, Cruyff turns . . . the lot. It showed you all of the building blocks of how to play soccer and gave each part a certain number; the higher the number the more complex the skill, and as you moved through the booklet, the skills got harder.

I must have been about 13 when I first got handed my booklet, and from the minute I got it, I never wanted to look at the last page to see what the final skill was. It may sound strange, but I've always been like that; I don't look up spoilers when I watch films or TV series, or when I'm reading a book. **THE ENTIRE TIME I WAS WORKING THROUGH THE BOOKLET, I WAS USING THIS FINAL PAGE AS MOTIVATION FOR MYSELF, TO DRIVE MYSELF TO COMPLETE THE BOOKLET FASTER. I WOULDN'T LET MYSELF LOOK AT THAT LAST SKILL UNTIL I'D MASTERED EVERY OTHER CHALLENGE IN THE BOOK.**

It wasn't easy, though. Every time I progressed to a new skill, at the back of my mind I was always thinking, "Why is this skill here and not at the back? What's at the back?!" I thought it might be something like how to combine loads of skills into one move, or showing me how to use my weak foot better, or working on my ability in the air.

I thought that whatever was at the end must be the hardest soccer trick of all time, and I used this knowledge to drive myself to be better. In my head, I had to be ready for whatever this final challenge was. And while I wanted to complete every other challenge in the book as quickly as possible, *I KNEW THAT I COULD ONLY GET TO THAT FINAL PAGE BY MASTERING EVERYTHING ELSE ALONG THE WAY.*

But learning all the skills in the booklet took a lot of time. And I mean a *lot*. It took hours and hours and *hours* of practice to become the soccer player I am today—and that's the thing a lot of people don't see: how every single part of my game took years to develop. It's the same for everyone you see playing soccer on television—every athlete I've ever met has put an incredible amount of time into practicing what they do. I know sometimes we're described as "naturally talented," but talent is only one ingredient in a much bigger recipe for success. In reality, it's all the time I spent on the sidelines, working on my soccer skills, doing kick-ups and working through that booklet that have got me to where I am today. I was just a small kid from Wythenshawe who didn't have much growing up, but with hard work and dedication, I've managed to achieve my dream. And if I can achieve my dreams, you can, too.

GOOD THINGS TAKE
TIME AND PRACTICE.
GOOD THINGS COME FROM YOU
DREAMING BIG, AND THEN
COMMITTING YOURSELF TO
TAKE STEPS TOWARD THAT
GOAL WHEREVER POSSIBLE.

YOU DON'T HAVE TO WORK ON IT ALL OF THE TIME,
BECAUSE OF COURSE THERE WILL BE TIMES WHEN YOU
GET TIRED OR WHEN YOU ARE STRUGGLING, BUT I
DO THINK IT'S IMPORTANT TO GIVE 100% WHENEVER
YOU'RE ABLE TO.

When I was going through that booklet, all sorts of different challenges
came up. One page asked me for the maximum amount of kick-ups
I could do, and all that practice around the semicircle when I was
younger meant I could already do that for three to four hours at a time.
Other skills were tougher to learn, but they all gave me a sense of
accomplishment when I finished them; I know that when
I've worked hard for something it means all the more
once I achieve it.

There was this one challenge, though . . .
I'll never forget it. The booklet asked
me to do **20 kick-ups, before
kicking the ball high in the
air and then controlling
it again on the half turn.**

The "half turn" is a soccer phrase for when you're taking the ball in motion—you're halfway through turning when you do it. It's a really important soccer skill to have, especially if you're an attacking player. If you're already turning instead of standing still or facing the ball when it travels to you, then you can play soccer a lot quicker. At the top level, being able to play quickly can be the difference between a **GOOD** player and a **GREAT** player.

When I'm taking a ball out of the sky, it's not enough that I balance it on my foot so that it doesn't fly in a wild direction. I have to take the ball and begin running with it straightaway—the idea is that while everyone is watching the ball and waiting to see what happens next, you've already figured out your next move and are racing away.

So picture me in my teens trying to do this challenge at United's academy.

The kick-ups I can do, as I've been practicing them for years. ✔

Kicking the ball high in the air, I can do that. ✔

Waiting for it to come down? Gravity takes care of that. ✔

Controlling it on the half turn? *THINGS GET A BIT TRICKY.*

The first few times I tried this skill were pretty hectic. I could do the kick-ups and take the ball down, but the difficult bit came from doing the half turn. Controlling a soccer ball while you're turning can be a bit like rubbing your stomach and patting your head at the same time—you're sending two different messages to your body at once. The very best soccer players see the ball in the air, decide which way they want to turn, and start the process before the ball even drops to them. It's really cool when you can do it properly.

But when I was starting out, one of two things used to happen:

1. I WAS TOO FOCUSED ON WATCHING THE BALL COME TO MY FEET, SO I HADN'T BEGUN THE PROCESS OF TURNING WHEN IT ARRIVED.

OR

2. I WAS TOO FOCUSED ON WHERE I WANTED TO TURN WITH THE BALL BEFORE IT ARRIVED, SO I DIDN'T CONTROL IT PROPERLY ONCE I HAD IT.

61

After a LOT of practice, I eventually managed to cross off the first problem—I would always make contact with the ball as I was turning, just a little bit, as the ball arrived at my feet. It was the second part, making sure the ball was properly under control, that proved difficult.

If you kick a ball up in the air, the first time it bounces off the ground will be the highest, the next will be a little lower, the next even lower, and so on.

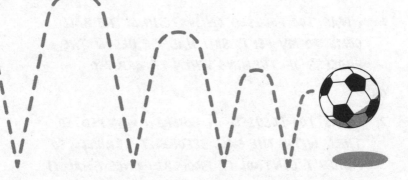

So when you want to control a ball that is falling, you want your first touch to take some of the speed off it. The best soccer players are described as taking a ball out of the air "stone dead" when they do this skill—they are able to take the bounce out of the ball in a single touch.

After tons of practice, I was able to get this skill down with my right foot okayish. The first touch was decent, and after a while, I managed to get the ball to go where I needed it to on the second touch. If I wanted to, I probably could have crossed off this challenge after a few days. The movement wasn't as smooth as I'd seen it done by the best soccer players, but it was okay for where the booklet said I had to be.

THE PROBLEM WAS I DIDN'T WANT TO BE AN "OKAY" SOCCER PLAYER. I WANTED TO BE ONE OF THE BEST.

So I decided to keep practicing the move again and again, until I could get it as smooth as some of my favorite players. Sometimes, when I'd get stuck on it, I would go on the computer and watch clips of players like **Ronaldinho**, **Cristiano Ronaldo**, **Wayne Rooney**, and **Lionel Messi**— those players all had great touches and could take the ball on the half turn. So I wanted to see how they did it, and studied them so I could do it, too.

YOU HAVE TO DREAM BIG AND THINK LONG TERM WHEN SETTING YOUR GOALS, BUT YOU ALSO HAVE TO HAVE THAT DRIVE TO GO OUT THERE AND CHASE IT.

I was practicing that skill when I was 13, telling myself I had to master it if I wanted to still be in the academy at 16. Then at age 16 I was telling myself that I wanted to be in the first team when I was 21. I managed to make my debut for United ahead of schedule, but that was thanks to many years of practice.

There's a saying that *LUCK IS WHAT HAPPENS WHEN YOUR PREPARATION MEETS THE RIGHT OPPORTUNITY*—the longer you spend practicing and working hard toward your goals, the luckier you'll end up being.

NOTHING IS PLAIN SAILING TO THE TOP. PROGRESS ISN'T A STRAIGHT LINE, AND YOU WILL ENCOUNTER DIFFICULTIES AS YOU WORK TOWARD YOUR GOALS.

There will be setbacks, rough patches, and times when you want to quit, tear it all up, and start again. Sometimes you'll get stuck, or run out of time, or you might get to what you think is your big moment but it doesn't work out the way you'd planned. But that's okay. I've been to Cup finals and won, but I've also been to a lot more semifinals and lost. *WHEN YOU COME UP SHORT IN A CHALLENGE, IT'S IMPORTANT NOT TO GIVE UP AND JUST STOP THERE, BUT TO LOOK AT WHAT HAPPENED AND THINK ABOUT HOW YOU COULD OVERCOME A SIMILAR PROBLEM IN THE FUTURE.* Think of all the hundreds and thousands of successful people in the world—they have all had to work really hard for what they want, but they have also failed *a lot* on their way.

One of my big sporting heroes is Muhammad Ali. He is the only boxer to have won the World Heavyweight Title three times, and was one of the first athletes to ever be called the **GREATEST OF ALL TIME**. I respect him a lot, not only for his boxing prowess but also for his strong beliefs—Ali believed in helping the people around you and uplifting those who needed it, and he fought for that both inside and outside of the ring. He once even had his title stripped from him because he refused to fight in the Vietnam War!

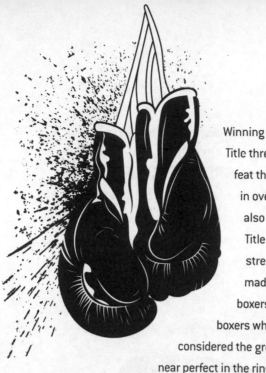

Winning the World Heavyweight Title three times is an incredible feat that no one has bettered in over forty years . . . but Ali also lost the Heavyweight Title twice. He had incredible strength and speed that made him one of the greatest boxers ever, but he still faced boxers who could defeat him. Ali is considered the greatest not because he was near perfect in the ring, but because he was amazing at how he bounced back when things went wrong, and stayed true to himself throughout.

IF YOU WANT TO BECOME THE BEST BOXER IN THE WORLD, YOU'RE GONNA GET PUNCHED IN THE FACE AND GET KNOCKED DOWN ALONG THE WAY. BUT WHEN THAT HAPPENS, IT DOESN'T MEAN THAT YOUR DREAM OF BECOMING THE WORLD HEAVYWEIGHT CHAMPION HAS GONE. IT JUST MEANS YOU'LL NEED TO LEARN TO TAKE THE GOOD TIMES WITH THE BAD.

I think about Ali and his stories a lot. He once said,

RECOGNIZE HOW
EVERY
MOMENT
OF OUR JOURNEY
IS AN IMPORTANT
PART OF THE
GROWTH
OF OUR SOUL

and it's a message that has stuck with me for years. It reminds me that even when we think we've failed, these failures are still an important part of our journey to success. I even put this quote on a pair of cleats for an England game once.

I'm not going to tell you that there is only one way to be successful in life, or that you **HAVE** to do one particular thing to get what you want. I certainly don't want you to go away thinking that you have to struggle for every moment in your life's journey. I practiced a lot on my path to becoming a soccer player, but I'm the sort of person who enjoys practice. You might not enjoy it all the time, and that's okay, too. I tend to wake up early to get my tasks done, whereas some of my friends like to wait until after lunchtime (I normally get a bit sleepy after lunch, so that's my time to relax!).

NOT ONLY IS IT IMPORTANT TO MAKE SURE YOU ARE **TRUE TO YOURSELF** AND YOU HAVE DREAMS THAT ARE **SPECIAL TO YOU**, IT'S ALSO IMPORTANT TO HAVE A PLAN THAT **WORKS FOR YOU.**

Everyone has different ways they like to study and learn. I've got friends who like to have things explained to them in books, while others prefer to listen to instructions. When I was at the academy, some players preferred being shown real-life examples, while other players learned best by practicing it first. Think about how you like to learn at school: Are you someone who prefers to solve problems through listening and speaking? Are you one for reading and making mind maps? Or do you like doing things yourself? There's no wrong way; what's most important is that you find what you like best, and try to do it as much as possible. (But don't make it the ONLY way you learn! It's important to have a mixture so you're always challenging yourself and staying open-minded. What you like to do in English class at age 14 might be completely different from how you like to learn math at age 16.)

FINDING OUT WHAT WORKS FOR YOU IS REALLY IMPORTANT, AS THAT CAN HELP YOU LEARN IN A WAY YOU LIKE BEST, WHICH WILL IN TURN HELP YOU FIND MORE OPPORTUNITIES FOR THINGS YOU'RE REALLY GOOD AT. When I was at school, I didn't really like asking the teacher questions. I'm not sure why, but I preferred to figure it out myself—almost as if I would memorize the lesson better that way. It sounds a bit weird now, but I guess it just shows that learning is different for everyone.

Whatever you're doing in life, you'll do it better when you're enjoying it, and you enjoy things more when you're learning and communicating the way that works best for you.
Do the things you enjoy and practice hard.
If you get stuck or stop enjoying something, take a break and come back to it when you feel fresher.

THIS IS YOUR JOURNEY, AND I WANT YOU TO DO IT YOUR WAY.

When I make a mistake, I find out where I went wrong, analyze it, and then I try to come up with a plan so that the next time I'm in a similar situation that mistake won't happen again. That was really important to me when I was learning how to take the ball on the half turn—I looked at the reasons why I was getting stuck and then slowly worked to get rid of each one step by step. I try to learn from my mistakes, but I don't want to think about them too much: When it's done, it's in the past, and there's no point looking backward. The only thing that's going to change is what you can do in the future, so keep your mind focused on what's ahead rather than on what you've already done. I like to think that keeps me humble, and that's really important to me.

If you're ever disappointed with a test result, or a game, or something else where you didn't do as well as you'd hoped, try to figure out what went wrong, but be kind to yourself when you are doing it. You're never going to be perfect, and even the best make mistakes. Take the positives where you can, look at what changes you can make to improve and focus on how you'll do it better next time. *THE MOST IMPORTANT THING TO REMEMBER IS THAT NO MATTER WHAT THE SETBACK IS, THERE IS ALWAYS A WAY BACK.*

You know that soccer skill I told you about? About taking the ball on the half turn? I got there in the end, but it took loads of practice (and loads of breaks from practice!) to learn how to do it in the way I wanted. And while I was really happy when I finally pulled it off, I didn't spend too much time patting myself on the back, as I had another page in the booklet to get to.

Getting to the end of that booklet was one of the biggest accomplishments of my teens. It was tough, but guess what my reward was when I was finished? Another bunch of challenges from another soccer coach!

THE STRANGE THING ABOUT ACHIEVEMENTS IS THAT YOUR HARD WORK CAN SET YOU UP FOR MORE CHALLENGES IN THE FUTURE. THINK OF IT AS FINISHING OFF ONE ADVENTURE AND THEN GETTING A WHOLE NEW ONE—honestly, if you asked me now what was on that final page, I'm not sure I could tell you!

Finishing that booklet was a big achievement for me when I was younger, because it became the foundation of other things in my life: like playing and scoring for Manchester United when I was 18, then winning the FA Cup a year later. Those achievements were big, and each one set me on new adventures, but I couldn't have got there if I hadn't put in all that practice along the way.

NEXT TIME YOU WATCH ME PLAY, SEE IF YOU CAN SPOT IT WHEN I TAKE A BALL OUT OF THE AIR. IT TOOK A LOT OF HARD WORK TO LEARN THIS, BUT I'M ALWAYS PROUD WHEN I PULL IT OFF. JUST FOR A LITTLE MOMENT, BEFORE I DO MY NEXT JOB.

1. BE YOUR OWN BEST COACH

You mostly hear the word "coach" in a sporting context. Perhaps you picture a coach standing at the side of a soccer field, shouting instructions at their players. In this vision, the coach needs to know more than the player—but in reality a coach is much more than that. The best coaches I have worked with stood out for three reasons: They believed in me, they asked me great questions, and then they listened to my thoughts and ideas to give me feedback. And guess what . . . you can learn to do those three things for yourself. Which is great, because the one person you spend the most time with is YOU.

To help you step into this mindset, have a think about these questions:

- When it comes to your dreams, what do you want to remind yourself of?

- How could you break your day down into small chunks to help you stay motivated?

- If you're struggling to believe in yourself, what would someone who did believe in you say?

- If you're having a bad day, what song or playlist will lift your spirits?

At the beginning of each day, look at yourself in the mirror. Make real eye contact with yourself for at least ten seconds. This sounds simple but it's actually quite hard (and it can even be quite funny!). As you look into your eyes, ask yourself:

- **What do you want your day to be like?**
- **What do you want to encourage yourself to try?**
- **What would you like to be like today?**
- **If something goes wrong, how would you like to encourage yourself?**

There are loads of other fun things you can try to coach yourself to make the most of each day. You could do it while you're tying up your laces, or put a hairband on your wrist and ping it gently to help yourself pay attention, or you could try to come up with your own strategy.

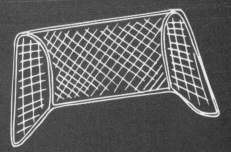

2. PREPARE FOR YOUR ADVENTURE

As I've shared in this chapter, my path to the soccer player I am today was not smooth. The path to your dreams never is, but the adventure is worth it.

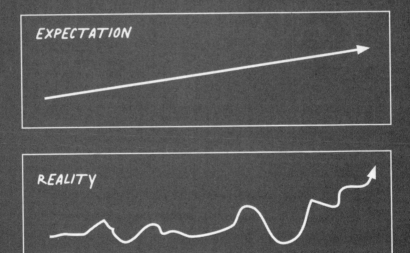

EXPECTATION

REALITY

To help you navigate the path, it can really help to think through a
few key things in relation to a goal you have:

- ❂ **What challenges might you face?**
- ❂ **How can you (a) prevent those challenges, or (b) manage them as best you can if they happen?**
- ❂ **When the going gets tough, what do you want to remember?**
- ❂ **Why do you care about this goal?**

WRITE DOWN YOUR ANSWERS TO THESE
QUESTIONS (AND ANY OTHERS YOU'D LIKE TO
ASK YOURSELF!) AND LOOK BACK AT THEM FROM
TIME TO TIME, TO KEEP MOVING TOWARD
YOUR DREAMS.

BUILD YOUR CONFIDENCE

4

DO YOU EVER GET NERVOUS?

I'm talking butterflies in the stomach. Big gulps. Your body feeling all shaky and stuttering over your words, nervous.

It can be the strangest feeling. One moment you're going about your day and the next:

You're like a deer in headlights, completely frozen by the world.

When I was at primary school, I used to get really nervous whenever I had to read out loud to the rest of the class. I was okay at reading to myself, in my head, where I could make funny voices and imagine far-off worlds, but when I was reading out loud . . . I don't know. I'd make more mistakes than usual, and it used to bother me. A lot.

WHEN YOU GET NERVOUS, YOU HAVE THIS THOUGHT THAT OTHER PEOPLE MIGHT SEE YOU WHEN YOU'RE NOT AT YOUR BEST, THAT THEY MIGHT THINK YOU'RE NOT CLEVER ENOUGH, OR NOT COOL ENOUGH, AND YOU WORRY ABOUT FEELING EMBARRASSED. When I was reading in my own head, there was no danger if I made a mistake, or had to repeat a page because I lost my place, but when I was reading out loud, my mind would start wandering, worrying that I was saying the words too fast or too slow, or that my classmates weren't enjoying it. When my mind did that, I wasn't focused on what was on the page—and that led to me making more mistakes.

I WAS NERVOUS BECAUSE I DIDN'T WANT TO LOOK SILLY IN FRONT OF MY CLASSMATES. AND THEN WHEN I DID LOOK SILLY—OR, I SHOULD SAY, WHEN I *THOUGHT* I LOOKED SILLY—I GOT MORE NERVOUS. I GOT CAUGHT IN A LOOP WHERE MY FEAR OF BEING EMBARRASSED LED TO ME BEING MORE EMBARRASSED.

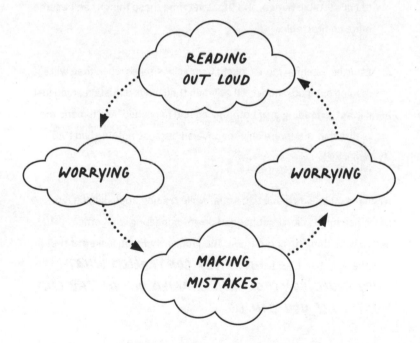

After a while, I got tired of it. Part of me wanted to duck out of view whenever the teacher was choosing someone to read aloud, but I knew that if I ran away from my problems they'd never go away. So I decided to do something about my nerves. I realized there were two positive steps I could take to get over my stage fright, which I would have to tackle piece by piece:

1. I needed to get out of my comfort zone. I started reading out loud more, sometimes in class and sometimes at home—whenever I got the chance. And in doing so I realized that I could do uncomfortable things, and that over time these things can become more comfortable.

2. I started listening more closely to my classmates when they were reading out loud. I noticed that when they made a mistake, they just carried on reading as if nothing bad had happened. And it made me realize that they were able to move on because nothing bad HAD happened.

When the other kids made a mistake while reading, they didn't fixate on it. Their minds didn't get bogged down, wondering what other people were thinking about them. They took a moment, looked at the mistake, and then they fixed it. *THEY CONTROLLED WHAT THEY COULD CONTROL AND CARRIED ON. IN THE END, THAT'S ALL YOU CAN DO.*

NERVES
STAGE FRIGHT
THE BUTTERFLIES
THE YIPS
THE HEEBIE-JEEBIES
THE BLUSHES

... THERE ARE LOADS OF WAYS TO DESCRIBE THE FEELINGS
YOU GET WHEN YOU'RE WORRIED ABOUT SOMETHING.

These feelings can appear in different ways, at different times, and they can affect us all for tons of different reasons. It's impossible to feel confident in everything you do—there are always going to be some things in life that you can do no sweat and other things that you might need more time to get comfortable with. I haven't felt nervous playing soccer in a long time, but that's because I've been practicing since I was four. But I DO get stressed out when I'm cooking. I've only started doing it recently, and I am so bad at making dinner when I'm already hungry—I get really hasty and start making **RASH MISTAKES**. Pun intended.

YEAH, THIS IS THE CHAPTER WHERE I ADMIT TO NOT BEING AS COOL AS I LOOK.

A lot of confidence is linked to practice. The more experience you have in something—whether it's in a sport, art, math, music, science, public speaking, or talking to new people—the more you know what you need to do for things to go right, and what you need to avoid so that things don't go wrong.

I KNOW IT CAN BE HARD—IT'S TOTALLY NATURAL TO WANT TO STAY IN YOUR COMFORT ZONE, WHERE YOU CAN CARRY ON DOING THE THINGS YOU KNOW HOW TO DO WELL, BUT IT'S ONLY BY GETTING OUT OF OUR COMFORT ZONE THAT WE CAN REALLY DEVELOP NEW SKILLS AND DISCOVER NEW AREAS OF LIFE.

One of my coaches at United used to say to me,

"IF YOU'RE NOT OUTSIDE YOUR COMFORT ZONE, YOU'RE DOING SOMETHING WRONG,"

and I think about that a lot during days when I'm on the fence about trying new things.

Even if you try something new and it doesn't go so well, you have to keep your chin up. Everyone is bad at something the first time they try it, but the people who are GREAT are there because they kept trying, so don't be put off if your first attempt doesn't go smoothly. If you want to be confident, it helps if you have experience; so if you end up out of your comfort zone every now and again, it might be useful to stay there for a bit and practice until the **uncomfortable** becomes **comfortable**.

In 2020, I stepped out of my comfort zone in a big way—I started campaigning about child food poverty and how we can do more to stop it as a community. A lot of people told me that I should "stick to sports," but I had found something I really cared about and I wanted to help to make a difference. I had a little experience on the subject because of my childhood, but it took practice to get confident using my voice to raise awareness of what was going on. I was really fortunate to talk to loads of incredible people who were also part of the campaign, and together our voices helped to make changes that we're all really proud of.

YOU MIGHT FEEL NERVOUS WHEN YOU FIRST STEP OUT OF YOUR COMFORT ZONE, BUT TRUST ME, IT WILL LEAD TO BRILLIANT THINGS.

But even saying all that, there are going to be times when you've put in all the practice and prepared as much as possible but you're still feeling nervous. I'll give you an example—it's the story of the last time I was properly nervous when playing soccer. I was 14 years old and had been called up to play for England's Under-16 team in a tournament called the Victory Shield. It was 2012, which was about the time I was beginning to realize that I might have a shot at being a professional player. I was doing well in training and getting noticed, and people were saying positive things about me.

IT WAS A GREAT FEELING, BUT IT ALSO MADE ME QUITE ANXIOUS. LIFE CAN BE STRANGE LIKE THAT; YOU CAN SPEND AGES WONDERING IF SOMETHING GOOD MIGHT HAPPEN, AND THEN WHEN IT DOES, INSTEAD OF ENJOYING IT, YOUR BRAIN CAN START WONDERING WHEN THE GOOD THING WILL STOP. Playing in the Victory Shield was one of the first **BIG** moments in my soccer career, but it didn't feel that way to me. Rather than enjoying it, I started worrying that it might be the only soccer moment in my career.

Back then I was suffering from something called Osgood-Schlatter disease, which is when your body is growing so quickly that you start to experience problems in your joints. Between the ages of 13 and 17 I used to have these horrible pains in my knees, which meant I wasn't allowed to play as much soccer as I wanted to. Although it was awful, I understood that my body was growing and I had to let it do its thing for a while. I could deal with the pain in my knees (sort of—it still really hurt at times), but I was so eager to get on the field that when I did get out there I overdid it trying to catch up with everyone else.

At the time, the Victory Shield was a tournament between the Under-16 teams of England, Scotland, Northern Ireland, and Wales. Our opening game was against Northern Ireland, and to be honest, I think it all got a bit much for me: the occasion, and the fact that I hadn't been playing as much as I would have liked. I was nervous and eager to impress, and it caused me to get lost in my own head. For the first ten minutes of that game, everything was going wrong for me; the ball kept going under my foot when I was trying to control it, my passes were going astray, I couldn't dribble or turn or shoot properly. I was getting so fixated on what was going wrong that I forgot all my processes for making things go right.

By halftime we were winning 1–0, but I was playing terribly. **I WAS DOUBTING MYSELF AND THINKING "YOU DON'T BELONG ON THIS TEAM"—WHICH IS NEVER A GOOD WAY TO THINK.**

One of my favorite phrases is

DO WHAT
BROUGHT
YOU
TO THE
DANCE

It reminds you to trust your talents when life takes you to new and
sometimes scary places; even though there are challenges ahead of
you, you've already got over loads of obstacles in the past to get to that
place. So if you get nervous before playing a final, you need to remember
that you got there because you won in a semifinal. If you trust your
talents and trust yourself, you can navigate anything.

There's also another great phrase,

DANCE WITH THE ONE WHO BROUGHT YOU

which is about remembering all the people who have helped you on your journey in life and saying thank you whenever possible. Oh, and there's **DANCE LIKE NOBODY'S WATCHING**, which is all about staying true to yourself and doing the things you enjoy, no matter what other people may think. There's just a lot of good bits of advice that relate to dancing!

I knew I had to do what brought me to the dance in that England game. I came out in the second half, and I went through all the simple parts of my game in order: I'd check my shoulders before I got the ball, I played simple passes, I only turned and ran into a space when it made sense.

These were all the small things that I'd been working on for years, but when I'd been nervous, I'd forgotten them. So I tried to beat my nerves by relaxing.

We ended up winning that game 5–0. I didn't play spectacularly in the second half, but by taking things back to basics and doing what I already knew well, I allowed myself to grow into the game.

That whole experience showed me I wasn't someone who played well if I thought too much about a big game. I just needed to remember that I was picked for that team for a reason, and I had a job to do.

There are loads of small little things about you that make you completely unique. When you get nervous and you're stuck thinking about all the things you can't do, it can be useful to pause for a little bit and go through all the things you know you can do to build your confidence back up. **TRY TO FOCUS ON ONE THING, HOWEVER SMALL, THAT YOU KNOW YOU CAN SORT OUT, AND TAKE THINGS FROM THERE.**

LIFE WILL THROW DIFFICULT SITUATIONS AT YOU AND YOU MIGHT FEEL A LOT OF PRESSURE WHEN THAT HAPPENS, SO IT'S IMPORTANT NOT TO ADD TO THAT BY WORRYING ABOUT THINGS THAT ARE OUT OF YOUR CONTROL.

It might sound silly, me telling you that I haven't been nervous playing soccer since I was 14, but I want you to trust me here. I know a lot of top athletes who use their nerves to pump themselves up before competing, and that can be a really positive thing for them, but that's not me. I realized that I'm not the sort of person who thrives off uncertainty and nerves, and that soccer, at the level I wanted to play at, was going to be full of high-pressure games. If I was going to be the soccer player I wanted to be, at the level I wanted to play at, I would need to perform consistently. I needed to find a way to take the pressure off myself before big games and not be nervous.

Before every single game I play, I remind myself of all the little things that make me, me. Of all the times I've faced challenges and come out the other side. I remind myself that I am where I am for a reason. It helps me to feel more confident so that I'm ready to go out and do what I need to do.

One of the things people say to young players who are trying to break through and play professional soccer at a senior level is "do whatever got you there, because nine times out of ten that's what's going to make you stay there." I think that's true of all aspects of life. So if you ever hear a voice in your head telling you that you're not good enough, *I WANT YOU TO STOP AND REMEMBER ALL OF THE AMAZING THINGS YOU'VE DONE AND THE CHALLENGES YOU'VE OVERCOME ALREADY TO GET TO THAT POINT. THINK ABOUT THE TIMES IN YOUR LIFE WHEN YOU GOT STUCK, AND THINK ABOUT HOW YOU GOT PAST IT.*

It might not come off instantly, but the next time you think "I'm not good enough" or start to doubt yourself, try to relax. Take a pause and try to get back to the things that you know you've done well in the past, then think about the things you're aiming to do in the future, and connect the two.

IT'S IMPORTANT TO REMEMBER THAT BUILDING YOUR CONFIDENCE SHOULDN'T MEAN YOU HAVE TO FAKE ANY PART OF YOURSELF, THOUGH. I still wear pretty much the same types of clothes now as I did when I was a teenager—it's what I feel most comfortable in and I've never really seen the point in copying others. Having confidence in yourself and knowing who you are is just as important as having confidence in new situations.

I was a shy kid at school, and I've always been dead nervous when it comes to making new friends. Growing up, all my friends were people who lived in my local area—we all went to the same school and hung out in the same parks—but later on, when I left home and went to digs with United, I lived in a different area with less-familiar faces, and things got a bit more difficult. I had to make new friends and meet different people from all sorts of backgrounds—new coaches, new teachers, new classmates—the lot. It felt weird for a bit, like I was speaking a different language from everyone else.

CHANGE CAN BE SCARY. DOING NEW THINGS CAN BE SCARY. EVEN GOING BACK TO OLD THINGS WHEN YOU HAVEN'T DONE THEM IN A WHILE CAN BE SCARY.

You might move house, or school, make new friends, or start learning a new skill—by the time this book makes it into your hands, we might be on our way out of lockdown. At times like that, it's easy for parts of your brain to start whirring, wondering things like, "Do people like me?" "Am I going to fit in here?" or "Am I good enough at this?" These questions can chip away at your confidence and make you doubt yourself, your dreams, and all the things you're doing.

Whenever you're in an environment where you might not know everyone or everything to a level you're comfortable with, you can end up asking questions about yourself. That's perfectly natural, but I think the big thing is trying not to put too much pressure on yourself when it happens.

A lot of life is about figuring things out: what you like, what you don't like, who you are, who you are trying to be and the people you want to spend your time with. It's one of those constant processes. And while that can be a lot, the best way to figure things out stays the same:

STAY TRUE TO YOURSELF

I KNOW I KEEP SAYING THAT (AND I WARN YOU, THIS ISN'T GOING TO BE THE LAST TIME!), BUT I REALLY MEAN IT. I WANT YOU TO KNOW THAT YOU'LL FIGURE IT OUT. THE PEOPLE YOU'RE MEANT TO BE FRIENDS WITH, WHERE YOU FIT INTO THINGS, ALL OF THAT STUFF WILL COME TO YOU IN TIME AS YOU GROW MORE CONFIDENT WITH WHO YOU ARE.

When I was growing up, I used to think that if I wasn't a shy person it would have sped up how quickly I settled into United's academy and high school. But no matter what happened, I've never been someone to shy away from who I am. The way I saw it, if someone was going to be my friend, it would be because they liked me for me. I didn't want to pretend to be someone different at the start and then have my friends get confused when they saw the real me—I knew it would be better if everyone knew who I was from Day One. Even though I may not have been the most confident person when meeting new people, I was confident in myself and knew I would figure it out one day.

BEING NERVOUS IS NATURAL, SO DON'T GET WORRIED WHEN YOU FEEL THAT WAY. IT'S GOOD TO TRY NEW THINGS, BUT REMEMBER THAT WHEN YOU DO GET NERVOUS, YOU DON'T HAVE TO DIVE IN HEAD-FIRST. IT'S FINE TO TAKE SMALL STEPS OUT OF YOUR COMFORT ZONE UNTIL YOU START TO FEEL COMFORTABLE AGAIN, AND THEN GIVE IT YOUR ALL WHEN YOU'RE READY.

If you've ever been to a swimming pool, think of it like how you get into the water. Some people dive in, while others prefer to get in slowly. It's okay if you're one of those people who prefer to dip your toe in to test the water—what's most important is you get into the pool eventually.

What you'll find is that the more you practice, the more you get used to the water. Bit by bit you'll go from one of those people who dips their toe in, to one of those people who can dive in no problem.

IT'S ALL ABOUT
GETTING CONFIDENT
IN YOUR SKILLS AND

PRACTICING

WHENEVER YOU CAN,
AND AFTER A WHILE
YOU'LL LEARN HOW TO
DIVE INTO
CHALLENGES LIKE
A CHAMPION

THE TRUTH ABOUT CONFIDENCE

The truth is, confidence comes and goes. Sometimes we feel confident and sometimes we don't. This is true for you and me, for famous actors, World Cup winners, Olympic champions, doctors, teachers, your parents . . . everyone.

Confidence can be influenced by lots of things, including:

- How difficult the challenge is
- Our previous experiences
- How much we listen to our doubts
- Who we have around us

Can you think of any other factors that influence your confidence?

Confidence is all about trust; self-confidence is having trust in yourself. You might be thinking, "Trust in myself to do what?" and if you are, that's a great question. The answer to that is our first key point.

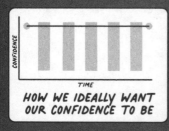

HOW WE IDEALLY WANT OUR CONFIDENCE TO BE

WHAT CONFIDENCE REALLY LOOKS LIKE . . .

1. TO BOOST YOUR CONFIDENCE, CHOOSE TO DEFINE SUCCESS AS "TRYING YOUR BEST"

This might sound really simple, but the best things in life often are. Imagine you have an exam coming up. You have two options:

Option 1: Define success as "passing the exam."

I understand you want to pass the exam but you can't control that. You can't guarantee it. Accepting what we can't control in life and focusing instead on what we can control is one of the most important life skills to learn. If you define success as passing the exam, you will probably be more nervous because your brain is wondering, "Will I or won't I pass?" and the honest answer is you don't know for sure. Where possible, our brains like to know things for sure.

Option 2: Define success as "trying your absolute best."
You can trust yourself to try your best, so this option will lead to you feeling more confident, and in turn that will lead to you performing better. It might take a bit of practice to think like this, but over time it will become more natural. To make this brain training work, it is really important for you to get clear on what "trying your best" involves. For me coming into a game, it means focusing on my

strengths, learning about the opposition, making good decisions in the week so I am ready in my body and my mind and then working hard in every moment for the team—whether I'm on the field trying to score goals, running back to defend, or sitting on the bench encouraging my teammates. When you define success like this, your brain knows you can do it, so you'll be more relaxed and perform better. It's a clever little mind trick—why don't you try it out?

Of course, it also means that after the exam, whether you pass or fail, as long as you can say "I tried my best" then you can hold your head up high. If you do fail, it's natural to be disappointed but you should still be proud because you can't do better than your best!

2. BUILD YOUR BELIEF

Have you ever noticed that your brain remembers the things that go wrong more than the things that go right? This is what psychologists call the "negativity bias." We have thousands and thousands of thoughts every day, and scientists think that up to 80% of them can be negative. These could be thoughts like worrying about something you did in the past, worrying about what might happen in the future, or comparing yourself to others. Many years ago, this thinking helped to keep our ancestors, cavemen and women, alive. They were more likely to learn from mistakes out hunting and think about where to find food. But for us today, it can make us a bit unhappy and anxious.

To tip the scales toward being more confident, we need to build our belief. To do this, think about the little successes you have had in life and the strengths you have within you. Try writing them out like the grid below—you could even stick them on your wall in your bedroom or on the mirror in the bathroom so you see it every day.

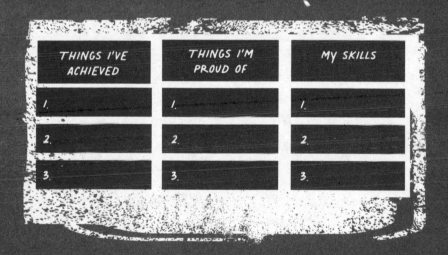

THINGS I'VE ACHIEVED	THINGS I'M PROUD OF	MY SKILLS
1.	1.	1.
2.	2.	2.
3.	3.	3.

3. CONFIDENCE IS A BEHAVIOR

Most people think about confidence as a feeling. To tell you the truth, so do I. We say: "I feel confident" or "I don't feel confident." I'm not a psychologist, but one thing I know for sure is that feelings come and go, I can shift my feelings, for example by listening to music I like, but I can't control them entirely.

So, if confidence is a feeling, then it makes sense that it will come and go, too. But there is another way to see it: I can choose to see confidence as a behavior and then choose to be confident in my actions.

Let's work with the example of having to give a presentation in front of your class. While some people might find this exciting, most people would probably feel quite nervous about it. This is because you care, and you want to do well. You have two options:

- **Option 1: Focus on how you're feeling, i.e., nervous, shaky, and try to control that. As you do that, you might find that you feel even more nervous!**

- **Option 2: Focus on what you need to do in order to feel confident, i.e., read the words slowly and clearly.**

Choosing the second option will help you to be in the moment and present well, even if you feel nervous. If you like the sound of this mind trick, here's a simple way to practice it in your life:

- Think about a situation you've got coming up for which you'd like to be confident.

- Imagine yourself feeling really confident in this situation. What would you be doing? What would someone see if they were watching you? What might you be saying to yourself?

- When you get into this situation, do the things you've just written down! Simple.

NO MATTER HOW YOU ARE FEELING, GO OUT THERE AND BEHAVE IN A CONFIDENT WAY. IF THE FEELINGS OF CONFIDENCE FOLLOW, THEN THAT'S GREAT. BUT EITHER WAY, YOU WILL HAVE DONE YOUR BEST, AND—AS YOU KNOW BY NOW—YOU CAN'T DO BETTER THAN YOUR BEST!

NAVIGATE
ADVERSITY

5

I WANT TO TELL YOU A LITTLE BIT ABOUT MY NANNA.

Nanna Cillian was one of the most amazing people I've ever met. I was really close with her when I was growing up, and practically lived at her house for six months when I was 7 years old. My mum was trying to get us to move house, so my brothers and I would all stay around Nanna's a lot while things got sorted.

My nanna was amazing. You know the type of person who seems to know everyone, knows where everything is and finds a way to make difficult things look really simple? That was her. She always thought ahead, had plans for everything, and was always looking out for me.

I have the best memories of her house. Every time I went over, it was full of all these different smells; there was coffee, cinnamon, nutmeg, and vanilla, all wafting through the place, and it was always full of laughter and happiness.

Every morning, after Nanna woke up, she would turn the kettle on, put something in the slow cooker for dinner and then start making cornmeal porridge. And this porridge was amazing. It takes a really long time to make properly, but it's worth it—it's one of the best things you will ever taste. If I ever spent the night at her house, she would usually give me some for breakfast, but this porridge was so good that whenever I had some downtime or got even a little hungry I'd be asking her if I could have some. It didn't matter what day of the week or what time of day it was, if I had been allowed to, I'd have eaten that corn porridge all day.

And while I'd get it for breakfast, most of the time when I asked she'd tell me I couldn't have it.

Which is odd, right? For a long time I was really confused by this—she's my nan, she loves me and looks out for me, but she wouldn't let me eat this porridge. I used to think the main reason was because it took so long to make—Nanna was a busy woman, and looking back, me asking for porridge all of the time was probably really annoying for her. She went weeks without explaining why she'd always say no, but one day she sat me down and told me her reasoning.

She said,

"IF YOU KEEP ASKING FOR THE SAME THING FROM THE SAME PERSON, YOU HAVE A LOT LESS CHANCE OF GETTING IT. IF YOU ASK THE SAME THING TO LOADS OF DIFFERENT PEOPLE, YOU'RE MORE LIKELY TO GET WHAT YOU'RE ASKING FOR."

Sounds a bit strange, doesn't it? But you have to understand my nanna was always imparting life lessons when you least expected it. Her explanation was about more than feeding me when I was hungry; it was her way of teaching me how to problem solve.

- **I had a problem: I wanted to eat porridge all the time.**

- **I tried solving it by asking my nan to make me some.**

- **When she said no, rather than figure out another way to get porridge, I kept asking her for it in the same way.**

Looking back, I probably should have tried some different strategies: I could have asked my mum or my brothers to make it for me, I could have traded chores in the house for it, or asked Nanna if she could teach me how to make it myself. Nanna was trying to get me to react and see if I'd try a different approach, and ever since then I've thought of corn porridge whenever I've been faced with a challenge.

IT REMINDS ME THAT YOU CAN'T DO THE SAME THING OVER AND OVER AGAIN IF YOU GET STUCK; YOU ALWAYS HAVE TO TRY TO HAVE MULTIPLE APPROACHES TO A SITUATION.

Nanna had this old Dell computer, and when I was staying with her, she would let me use it to look up soccer clips. After school, I'd do my homework and any help she needed around the house, and then I'd be straight on YouTube or the BBC. At the time I had two favorite players, Wayne Rooney and Cristiano Ronaldo, and I would watch both of them do soccer skills repeatedly, and then I'd practice those skills around the house. But after my nan told me how it's better to ask the same thing from different people, I started to change my approach.

I was watching all these soccer clips to learn how to become one of the best players in the world, but I realized that I'd only learn so much by watching the same two people over and over again. If I wanted to get what I was asking for, I'd be better off asking the same

question to lots of different soccer players—not just my favorites, but ALL of the greats. How did the best players in the world do the things they did?

I started watching clips of Thierry Henry, Ronaldinho, Lionel Messi, Paul Scholes . . . loads of different types of players. I wanted to understand what was going through their heads, not only so I could learn from them, but also so I could learn how to beat them. I'm not a defender, but I even watched clips of center-backs like Paolo Maldini, because I thought that if I studied how top-level defenders played I'd learn how to get past them on the field.

My nan refusing to give me that corn porridge was one of those tiny moments that had a big impact on me. It taught me this lesson:

THERE'S ALWAYS MORE THAN ONE SOLUTION TO A POTENTIAL PROBLEM

You will face all sorts of problems in life—big ones, small ones, problems that you can solve really quickly and other problems that will last a lot longer—and you will make mistakes. Sometimes you will fail in what you're trying to achieve, even when you put in the hard work and do everything in your power to reach your goal. But that's okay—success isn't always guaranteed. Trust me, I fail at something nearly every day.

I know it might seem like I'm making things up, but my life is FULL of mistakes—as a profession, soccer depends on them! If everyone did their job properly 100% of the time, then every game would end 0–0. And everyone, from the players to the fans, would be bored.

When my team scores a goal, it's usually because the opposition has made a mistake, and on the flip side, if my team concedes a goal, it's probably because we've made a mistake. If I add up all the games of soccer I've played—from the park, to the playground, to the academy, to the senior team, and international duty—I will have made thousands of mistakes, and I've watched other people do the same. It's impossible to play a perfect game of soccer; you will always end up making mistakes and encountering problems.

WHAT YOU CAN DO, THOUGH, IN BOTH SOCCER AND IN LIFE, IS LEARN HOW TO RECOVER FROM SETBACKS.

IT'S OKAY TO MAKE MISTAKES AND FOR THINGS TO GO WRONG; WHAT'S MORE IMPORTANT IS THAT YOU HAVE THE RIGHT RECOVERY FROM IT. IF YOU REACT TO A SETBACK WELL, NOBODY WILL REMEMBER THE MISTAKE.

In 2018 I went to Russia to play in the FIFA World Cup with England, and in our knockout game against Colombia, in Round 16 of the competition, we were winning by a goal for most of the game. Knockout games can be really tense, and it's a massive advantage to score first—we were ahead and looked in control . . . until we conceded a goal in the 93rd minute. Soccer games are 90 minutes long, so you are not meant to let the other team score in the 93rd minute of a game that you are winning. But we made a mistake, which meant that rather than go through to the quarter-finals, we had to play another half hour of soccer in extra time and then eventually play penalties.

England doesn't have the best track record in penalties. Before 2018, we had never won a penalty shootout in a World Cup. So we had a BIG problem.

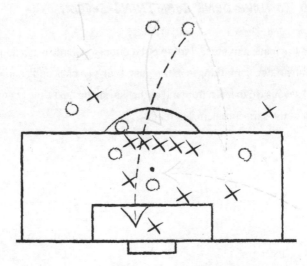

A lot of people thought we were going to crumble under the pressure, but we managed to collect ourselves and decided we weren't going to let a mistake be the end of our World Cup journey. The coaches told us what to expect in extra time and told us to be brave, so when we got to the penalties, we stepped up in the big moment and supported each other. And then, eventually, after two hours of play and a penalty shootout, we beat Colombia to get to the next round. Nowadays most people don't even remember that Colombia scored in the 93rd minute—they mostly remember how we stayed firm in the penalty shootout and won.

We didn't win the World Cup, but we got to the semifinals, and when we got home, a lot of soccer fans said we had achieved something incredible in Russia. *IT REALLY GOT ME THINKING THAT YOU DON'T ALWAYS NEED THE GOLD MEDAL AT THE END TO HAVE DONE SOMETHING SPECIAL.*

Once I've made a mistake, I try to put it out of my mind as quickly as possible. Once something is in the past, I can't go back and change it. But I always try to learn from my setbacks, so the next time I come up against the same problem, I'm ready.

Or at least I try to be ready. Like I've said before,

SOMETIMES YOU MAY FAIL IN THE THINGS YOU LOOK TO ACHIEVE, **AND THAT IS OKAY.**

In my career, I've played in a lot of important games and won. I've also played in a lot of important games and lost. It's all part of the journey.

NOW, I DON'T LIKE TO ADMIT THIS, BUT WHEN OTHER TEAMS BEAT MY TEAM OR WIN A TROPHY WE WERE COMPETING FOR, SOMETIMES I GET JEALOUS. I TRY NOT TO BE JEALOUS FOR TOO LONG (REMEMBER WHAT I SAID ABOUT COMPARING YOURSELF TO OTHERS!), BUT I MIGHT BE HARD TO FIND FOR A LITTLE BIT. I'M NOT A SORE LOSER OR ANYTHING, BUT I LIKE TO BE ALONE OR WITH MY SMALL CIRCLE OF FRIENDS AND FAMILY, SO YOU WON'T SEE ME ON SOCIAL MEDIA AT TIMES LIKE THAT.

I can't be a sore loser in what I do because I know what it takes to win. The way I see it, if another team wins something at the expense of me or my team, they deserve to win. I'm not the only person dedicating myself to my training and my goals, so of course I'm going to come up against people who have put in just as much effort as me and my teammates. Sometimes I'll win, and sometimes I'll lose. It's happened to me both ways before, so that's why I understand it.

My brothers always used to say to me:

"WHEN YOU GO OUT ON THE FIELD, GIVE 100%. THAT WAY YOU WILL WALK OFF THE FIELD WITH YOUR HEAD HELD HIGH, WIN, LOSE, OR DRAW, BECAUSE YOU'VE DONE THE ABSOLUTE MOST YOU CAN FOR YOURSELF, FOR THE TEAM AND FOR THOSE WHO COUNT ON YOU. THE MOST YOU CAN DO IN THIS LIFE IS TRY YOUR BEST."

That's a lesson I've taken outside the game and into everything I do. (Especially when I'm cooking!)

Sometimes the best way to deal with a setback is by getting back up, dusting yourself off and then immediately going back to the situation with more effort. Sometimes you need to take a break to come up with a new plan so you can return to it later. Other times you might need help to get back up, or to dust yourself off. Sometimes the best thing you can do is say "Well done" to the person who beat you.

RIGHT NOW is the best time for you to learn; your brain is a sponge and you will pick things up quickly, but that also means you're going to make a lot of mistakes as you figure everything out. You're going to learn all about what I like to call "the good mistakes," which are mistakes we make on the road to getting good at something.

I'll give you an example. I'm trying to learn both Spanish and Italian, and sometimes I get them mixed up when I'm talking. To me the two languages seem really similar, and I can get the wires crossed in my brain, so when I'm talking to someone at United or to a journalist from another country, sometimes I make a mistake and talk in a different language. But most of the time when it happens, the person on the other end will kindly show me where I went wrong so I can get it right next time. *A GOOD MISTAKE IS SOMETHING THAT SHOWS YOU HOW YOUR BRAIN WORKS AND WHAT TO DO NEXT, SO YOU'RE LESS LIKELY TO MAKE THAT SAME MISTAKE AGAIN. YOU'RE GOING TO MAKE PLENTY OF THOSE IN YOUR LIFE, AND IT'S GOING TO BE OKAY—IT PROVES THAT YOU'RE LEARNING.*

And the older you get, the more good mistakes you'll make. One of the tricky things about growing up is that everything scales along with you. Just a little. As you get better at navigating challenges, the challenges get bigger and more complex for you. Nothing is smooth sailing, and you won't reach a certain age where everything suddenly becomes perfect, but what you can do is what my nanna showed me: learn to ask loads of people for advice and help whenever you can. You can go a long way if you pick up lots of different ways to approach challenges.

My soccer career is only going to get more difficult—the more I play in big games, the more likely I am to lose big games, just as much as win them, so it's important for me to carry all the little lessons and details I've picked up along the way.

SOMETIMES THINGS GO IN YOUR FAVOR, AND WHEN THEY DO YOU SHOULD FEEL PROUD AND CELEBRATE

Other times things won't go your way, and that's when it's important to

RECOVER, RESET, AND KEEP WORKING HARD

until things get back on track. I'm getting better at learning to be kind to myself when I have a setback, but that's because I've been through the experience of making mistakes.

Nanna Cillian passed away when I was 11 years old. I'm not going to dress this bit up—it was a terrible time in my life. I was moving out of home to go to digs and this amazing woman, who had looked after my mum and my brothers and my sisters and me, was suddenly gone.

SOMETIMES YOU CAN LOSE SOMEONE AND GO THROUGH THINGS THAT YOU'RE NOT GOING TO RECOVER FROM IN THE SAME WAY. THERE MIGHT BE MOMENTS IN YOUR LIFE OF IMMENSE PAIN AND SADNESS, AND I'M REALLY SORRY IF YOU'VE HAD TO GO THROUGH THAT ALREADY. There are some things that planning and questioning and hard work just can't fix. In times like those, what gets you through are the people around you. Because there will always be people around you, no matter how dark things may seem.

I remember the sadness in my family's eyes when we went to Nanna's funeral, but I also remember the smell of her corn porridge and all of the lessons she taught me, big and small. Next time you see me playing soccer, check out what I do before I get on the field: I always do the sign of the cross, and then I point up to my nanna. She never got to watch me play, but I know she's a part of me, and I always try to say something to her before a game.

I remember the lessons she taught me, tap my cleats four times before I step on the field—which is my little routine I do to keep focused— and then I know I'm ready to go out there and give it my best. That's my way of trying to share what big moments I can with her, even though she is gone.

There will be hardships in life, big and small, and I'm sorry about that. But there will be big moments of joy in your life as well, and I think it's really important you try to look to the people around you in both the good and bad moments when they arrive. You're never alone in this life, and I know my nanna is proud of me and the things I am doing, always. I wouldn't be here without her, and I try to carry all of her lessons with me, no matter what I do.

IF YOU GIVE IT YOUR ALL WHENEVER YOU CAN, YOU MIGHT SURPRISE YOURSELF WITH WHAT CHALLENGES YOU'LL BE ABLE TO GET THROUGH AND HOW YOU CAN HELP OTHERS.

I PROMISE YOU THAT YOU WILL
ACHIEVE AMAZING THINGS. TRUST
ME, I EVEN STARTED TO LEARN
HOW TO MAKE CORN PORRIDGE
THE OTHER WEEK.

1. THE F WORD!

Have a go at this word game and see what you notice. Did you find that a word just popped into your head at the end of the list?

FILL IN THE MISSING WORD	NOW FILL IN THE MISSING WORD
1. Red	1. Plum
2. Blue	2. Nectarine
3. Orange	3. Pear
4. Yellow	4. Apple
5. Gr _____	5. Gr _____

Our brains do this all the time, filling in the blanks and coming up with creative ways to tell stories. Now think about the word "failure." Close your eyes and picture it in your mind. When you see or think about that word, what thoughts and feelings come to you? Write down three, then have a look at the words you wrote down.

Are they positive? If you're anything like me, you probably wrote down things like "disaster," "bad news," or "embarrassing." We tend to think of failure as a problem, but here's the truth: Failure can be our friend. I really mean it. Failure can be our friend if it means we pushed ourselves out of our comfort zone, if we did our best, if we can learn from it.

With this mindset, choose three more words or phrases to describe how you want to think and feel about failure. Here are mine:

- 🌀 **A chance to grow**
- 🌀 **Learning**
- 🌀 **Proof I pushed myself**

2. CELEBRATE MISTAKES!

To help you really step into the mindset that failure can be a good thing, it's now time to think about your own experiences. Write down two things you have failed at in life so far. When you've done that, think about these questions:

- 🌀 **What did these failures teach you?**
- 🌀 **How are you stronger for these setbacks?**
- 🌀 **Despite failing, did you try your best with the skills you had and in the circumstances you were in at the time? If the answer is yes, maybe you didn't fail . . . Maybe you did your best, and you just need to keep working to make your best better.**

6

I HAVE A BIT OF A CONFESSION TO MAKE. TO BE HONEST, I WASN'T TOO SURE IF I WAS GOING TO SHARE THIS STORY WITH YOU, BUT THEN I STARTED WRITING THE BOOK AND ONCE I GOT INTO THE FLOW OF THINGS, I REALIZED IT MIGHT BE INTERESTING FOR YOU TO READ.

So . . . I wasn't always a well-behaved kid. Nothing too naughty, though—mostly cheeky, rather than anything else. My mum used to tell me off if I was rude or told a lie, but every now and then I'd play this game with my friends called "Knock a Door and Run"—it's where you knock on someone's front door and run away before they can answer it. (It's a really silly game, and looking back now, I have no idea why my friends and I used to play it when there were other—way more fun—ways to spend our time!)

KNOCK KNOCK

There was one house in the area that belonged to a really serious man who didn't like practical jokes very much. He wasn't someone you messed with, so no one would ever knock on his door—none of us wanted to see him get angry or for him to call our parents. We were all too scared. (See? More cheeky than naughty!) But one night we were feeling really cheeky for some reason, and we decided that tonight was the night. We took it proper seriously and planned everything, even the escape route we'd take after knocking on his door. I was going to do the actual knocking (I was always the one who knocked because I was the fastest), and then we were going to run down the road and cut through to one of the canals close by so he wouldn't be able to catch us. Honestly, I cringe a bit when I remember how much time we spent planning this practical joke.

When it's evening time, we go through the plan one last time. Then all my friends take their places by the front gate of the house, ready to run at a moment's notice. I walk up to the front door (proper nervous) and get ready to knock. *PICTURE IT LIKE ONE OF THOSE CARTOONS: I KNOCK ON THE DOOR THREE TIMES AND BEGIN REVVING UP MY FEET TO RUN AWAY AS SOON AS I HEAR FOOTSTEPS—BUT WHEN I STARTED TO RUN, I JUST FELL OVER! FLAT ON MY FACE. I MUST HAVE HAD MY SHOELACES UNTIED OR SOMETHING.*

I knew that I was done for. This man was coming to answer his front door, and he wasn't going to be too happy about me and my friends bothering him. He was going to find me lying there, and he would know that I was trying to play a prank. My feet didn't work, but my mind started racing, thinking about all the trouble I was going to get into: He was going to yell at me, tell my mum, and I was going to get grounded. For a minute there, I'm sure I shut my eyes, just waiting for the front door to open.

But instead, I felt one of my friends grab my arm and pull me up. Turns out that when all my friends saw me fall over, rather than burst out laughing or just leaving me there to get into trouble by myself, they decided to pick me up and get me out of there. We had to redirect our route, but we got away without the very serious man realizing what had happened. It was close, though. My heart was racing, but I don't think anyone in the area knew what had happened apart from my friends. (And now all the people reading this. Whoops!)

If I ever played this game on your house when I was a kid fifteen years ago, I'm really sorry. I'm not telling this story because I want you to think "Knock a Door and Run" was cool, but because I want to share with you a little bit about my friends. Ever since we were kids, we've always tried to help and support each other whenever we can. We always try to pick each other up; through the good times, the bad times, and even the silly times when we do things we should never **(EVER)** do again.

There's this saying that goes:

IF YOU WANT TO GO FAST, GO ALONE BUT IF YOU WANT TO GO FAR, GO TOGETHER

So far in this book, **I** have been speaking to **YOU**. It's been a one-on-one conversation about my hopes for you on your life's journey. But this is the part where I'm going to use the word **WE** a lot more, because I wouldn't be able to do the things I do in my life without an incredible group of family and friends around me.

We should start by talking about my mum, Melanie. She is an unbelievably strong woman. Sometimes I cannot put into words how much I love her (but I'll try my best here). My mum has been through some of the worst things that you could imagine, but she has never let anything that's happened take away her smile. When I was growing up, she worked three jobs and ran a house with my siblings and myself running about the place, and she still found time to give us so much love and good advice. She always tries to see the bright side of things, which is something I'm so lucky to have learned from her.

I OFTEN GET ASKED, **WHO IS THE TOUGHEST PERSON YOU KNOW?**

IN SOCCER INTERVIEWS, AND I THINK PEOPLE ALWAYS EXPECT ME TO SAY ANOTHER PLAYER. BUT MY ANSWER EVERY SINGLE TIME IS

MY MUM.

She's not a big soccer person, but every night before a match, she'll always call to give me a little pep talk. It's the same piece of advice every time—go out and enjoy it and if you play well you'll win the game—but she's right. My mum is always right. She's one of the best people I can speak to before I play, because she knows exactly what I need to hear in order to be ready. She always knows the right words to say.

There's a lot of my mum in me (and I don't just mean we look alike!). She has passed on so many traits that are really important to the way I live my life.

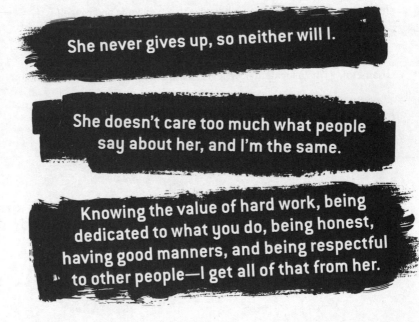

She never gives up, so neither will I.

She doesn't care too much what people say about her, and I'm the same.

Knowing the value of hard work, being dedicated to what you do, being honest, having good manners, and being respectful to other people—I get all of that from her.

But the best lesson she has taught me is to

ALWAYS APPRECIATE EVERYTHING

because she knows that life isn't easy. There are so many things that can go wrong, and she taught me

NOT TO LET THE BAD THINGS DEFINE WHO I AM.

That's a lesson I want you to take from this book as well.

WHATEVER YOU ARE DOING IN LIFE, NO MATTER WHERE YOU MIGHT END UP, IT'S GOOD TO HAVE SOMEONE YOU CAN TRUST ALONGSIDE YOU. SOMEONE WHO YOU KNOW BELIEVES IN YOU. THAT PERSON MIGHT BE YOUR MUM, YOUR DAD, YOUR GUARDIAN, A TEACHER, OR A DIFFERENT ADULT. IT COULD BE A SIBLING, OR IT COULD BE A FRIEND. IT COULD BE ANYONE. WHAT MATTERS IS THAT THERE IS SOMEONE OUT THERE WHO IS ROOTING FOR YOU AND WHO WANTS EVERYTHING TO WORK OUT FOR YOU.

YOU ARE NEVER EVER ALONE IN THIS LIFE

EVEN THOUGH THERE MIGHT BE TIMES WHEN YOU FEEL LONELY, THERE IS ALWAYS SOMEONE OUT THERE WHO WILL HELP YOU WHEN YOU'RE HAVING A TOUGH TIME. THERE'S ALWAYS SOMEONE WHO WANTS YOU TO BE YOURSELF, WHO WANTS YOU TO TRY YOUR

HARDEST AND WHO WANTS TO SEE YOU HAPPY.
EVEN IF YOU DON'T ALWAYS SEE IT, OR IF THAT
PERSON IS A LITTLE HARD TO FIND, THERE WILL
ALWAYS BE SOMEONE TO GRAB YOUR HAND IF YOU
ARE REACHING OUT. I PROMISE.

MY MUM is one of those people for me, and I'm really blessed to have her. She has always believed in me and has taught me loads of important lessons throughout my life. Now that I'm older, I'm passing on those lessons to my younger family members and the next generation. That's why you're reading this book right now—because I want you to know that I believe in you, too.

MY BROTHERS, Dwaine and Dane, didn't like to admit it, but they were always watching over me, whether it was in the garden, at the park, or in my games when I was younger. When he was a teenager, Dwaine's motivation to learn how to drive was because he wanted to take me to soccer lessons! They're still watching out for me now, still giving me loads of advice about how to get better at soccer, how I can grow as a person, and what I can do next. I'm a big man now, but I'm never too big for advice from them, and they're never too busy to help me out.

MY SISTERS, Chantelle and Claire, also showed me a lot growing up. I didn't always share a house with them because they're older than me, but I love them the same way I love my mum. They have the same strength that she has, and they both spent a lot of time protecting me and making sure I was on the right path. It was my sisters who showed me how to be funny, how to make friends with new people at school, and how to make sure I look after all of my friends. They now have their own children, and watching my sisters pass on those same lessons to my nephews is the most incredible thing.

MY COUSIN Sabrina was the busiest person I knew when I was a child, but she always made time for family and would check up on me because she said that was important. Now that I'm older, I try to do the same thing and make time for the people who are important to me.

I even used to think that **MY SCHOOLTEACHERS** gave me so much work because they didn't want to see me happy, until I realized they were just trying to give me the tools I needed to achieve my dreams when the time came.

There are always going to be people all around you who want you to do well. Not just family, but friends, too. I think that when you have a good friend, someone who you know is really special, they can be just as important.

YOUR FRIENDS CAN BE THE FAMILY YOU CHOOSE FOR YOURSELF

I have three really close friends that I want to tell you about. We met in a really fun way. I must have been about 7 years old and my mum, my brothers, and I had just moved house. It was the school holidays, and I was sitting at home, not doing much, when I heard a knock on the door. When I answer it there's this boy, the same age as me, holding a soccer ball and asking if his friend was home.

He told me his name was Jamie. Jamie was looking for his friend who had lived in the house before me—turns out they had moved out and not told him! When Jamie found this out, he thought it was funny, and then he turned around to leave. But you should know me by now: If I see a soccer ball, I'm going to try and play.

So I did. I said,

ER, ARE YOUSE GOING TO PLAY SOCCER?

And then he replied,

YEAH, YOU CAN COME IF YOU WANT.

And that was that.

We went to the park, and from then on, we went out every single day together. Jamie is such a fun, chilled-out guy. My sisters used to give him all sorts of nicknames, and he'd just laugh and smile when he heard them. He introduced me to another one of his really good friends, Ashley, and we became close, too. Ash was a really good soccer player (actually, he still is now!), and he was always playing down at the park. He loves all the little details of the game, just like me, so whenever I learned a new soccer trick, he'd be the first person I'd show. He's really competitive, and he's got a heart of gold—he wouldn't wish anything bad on anyone, and that's something I really like about him.

For ages Jamie, Ashley, and I were inseparable. We'd walk to school together, walk home together, and then go play in the park. A little later on, we met this lad called Roshaun, and he joined our gang. I'm still friends with all of them, but honestly I don't really see them as friends anymore—they're so special to me that they're basically my other family. I can share the same things with them I'd share with my mum or my siblings, and they know they can trust me, too. Their friends often became my friends, and their families became my family. Ashley's twin sister, Abby, used to join us on our adventures in the park and playing soccer—she fit right in because a friend is a friend no matter what form they come in. She was the sensible one, and she showed me from an early age that girls could do anything boys could do, and I'm forever grateful. I even call Ashley's mum my second mum—when I go round their house she tells me to help myself to anything I need, and I make her cups of tea and everything.

DURING YOUR LIFE, YOU'RE GOING TO MEET PEOPLE WHO WILL CHANGE YOUR LIFE. PEOPLE WHO WILL BE ABLE TO MAKE YOU LAUGH WITH JUST A GLANCE, WHO CAN HELP YOU FEEL SAFE AND WHO CAN OPEN UP THE WORLD FOR YOU. I'VE HAD FRIENDS WHO HAVE INTRODUCED ME TO THE MUSIC I LIKE NOW, WHO HAVE TAUGHT ME IMPORTANT LIFE SKILLS AND WHO HAVE INTRODUCED ME TO OTHER AMAZING PEOPLE.

I'm so thankful for my friends. It may sound a little strange, but every now and then, I feel like I can be a bit difficult to be around: I can be disorganized at times, or I can talk about soccer too much, and when people talk to me for the first time, I get a bit worried that I'm not always making sense. I might go "er" a lot and take long pauses when you ask me a question. I'm not trying to be rude, but I say "er" to give myself time to think. Trust me, though, if you're talking to me, I am paying attention, I just might not show it in the most obvious way. It can take time to get used to me, and my friends understand all these things about me and love me anyway. And I understand them and love them back. **WHEN YOU'RE SURROUNDED BY GOOD FRIENDS, ALL THE WORRIES YOU HAVE ABOUT YOURSELF TEND TO MELT AWAY, BECAUSE THEY REMIND YOU THAT THOSE LITTLE THINGS DON'T MATTER IN THE END.**

One thing I love about Jamie, Ashley, and Roshaun is how they've all remained the same happy, smiling, good-natured people since we were kids. They've never treated me any differently in all the years I've known them. Not back then, when I didn't have much, and not now things are different. It's still the same kindness and the same jokes, and it makes me want to act the same way for them. My life has been a bit of a roller coaster, but they've been with me all the way.

YOU'RE GOING TO MAKE FRIENDS JUST LIKE THAT.
PEOPLE WHO UNDERSTAND AND LOVE ALL THE LITTLE
THINGS YOU DO THAT OTHER PEOPLE MIGHT FIND
STRANGE. IT MIGHT BE HARD TO SEE IT NOW, AND
IT MIGHT NOT HAPPEN TODAY, OR TOMORROW, BUT
IT WILL HAPPEN ONE DAY AND IT WILL FEEL AMAZING.

They'll think your jokes are funny, and they won't mind if you're talking about soccer or any of your other hobbies (yet again!) because they know it makes you happy. That's what makes a friend special, and what makes them like family—when they appreciate you and want to see you happy. For me, a friend is someone who I always want to see happy, because that makes me happy, too.

I also want to know my friends are safe. We always look after each other and pick each other up when we fall (and not just when we are playing silly games!). Growing up, Jamie, Ashley, and Roshaun would help my siblings and my mum keep me on the right path in my journey. If there were parties that I wanted to go to, but I had soccer or school work to catch up on, they would be there with me to make sure I stayed focused. Without their help, my life and career would've gone a completely different way.

If I was ever going out, my mum would tell me to

STAY WITH YOUR FRIENDS, KEEP YOURSELF TO YOURSELF, AND DON'T GET IN ANY TROUBLE.

And that's stuck with me a lot. If I'm doing something that I feel really passionate about, my friends will support me and look out for me—and that works both ways.

My friends and my family are often my motivation; I've always wanted to make my mum proud, so when she tells me she's proud of me, that makes me so happy. It still motivates me now—of course I still want to win soccer trophies and do other things in my life, but deep down, I want to make my family and friends proud more than anything. It's really important to me that I use the lessons my mum taught me, always try my best and look out for people. That's why I'm always building connections with other people who can help me do this.

There's one person in my life now, Kelly, who is almost like an extra big sister. She helps me organize things that are important to me, and introduces me to other people who can help me achieve the big things I want in life. That helped a lot when we were campaigning in 2020.

When lockdown first happened and I learned that a lot of children weren't going to get the support they might have got from breakfast clubs and free school meals, I was really concerned. When I was growing up, going to breakfast club before school really helped me; not just because there was food there, but because it showed me that there were people out there who cared and would look after people like me. Breakfast club was more than a place I went to before I started my morning lessons; it was a place where I learned a lot about the world. So I wanted to find a way to make sure children were getting the support they needed, not only through the school holidays, but for as long as possible.

I wasn't an expert on school meals and vouchers when I started campaigning in March 2020. My initial plan was to help those in breakfast clubs and community centers get the meals they needed over the holidays, but as I started to learn more about the situation, I became more and more passionate about helping out. I wanted to make a difference. Through Kelly, I met other people who were passionate about the same issues and who KNEW how to make a difference. From there, our network got bigger and bigger, until we had a whole team of passionate people, experts, volunteers, and politicians all working together to help make a change. When you get loads of people together who are all working toward a single cause, the most phenomenal things are possible. We all became champions for this cause, which was helping to get food to and support the children who needed it most.

THAT'S MY DREAM: TO DO THAT OVER AND OVER AGAIN IN LOADS OF DIFFERENT WAYS, TO HELP AS MANY PEOPLE AS I CAN. I WANT EVERYONE TO FEEL AS IF THEY HAVE A NETWORK OF FRIENDS, FAMILY, AND SPECIAL PEOPLE THEY CAN CALL UPON DURING THEIR JOURNEYS.

Your friends, your family, everyone who's important to you—they all have a massive part to play in your life and can help form the foundation of the person you want to be. Your life is your own journey, but make sure you always pay attention to those who help you along the way—through good times as well as the bad—and be thankful for that help. Appreciate the people who are there for you, and try to be there for them in return. When we build strong connections with people like that, amazing things can happen.

1. WHO IS IN YOUR TEAM?

Have you ever thought about the amount of people you will meet in your life? I guess it's impossible to know, but some scientists think it could be more than 10,000! That's a lot of people, and only a select few will be in your team.

I like the saying that we meet people for "a reason, a season, or a lifetime." It can be fun to think about who you have met for a particular reason (maybe you learned something important from them or you were able to make a difference in their life), and who you'd like to be with you for a lifetime. One thing I know for sure is that to help you be the best you can be, it's really important to get your kind of people in your team.

To help you think about your team, here are a couple of questions for you:

> Of the people you currently spend time with, who would come and pick you up if you tripped over and fell? Once you've worked that out, spend more time with them—they probably want the best for you, and that's a very good thing.

Who do you value? Who is helping you grow? Write their names down in a notebook and then think about what they stand for. What do they teach you by the way they live their life? For me— as you know by now—it would be my mum, my brothers, my sisters, the rest of my family, my friends, and so many others. I really love thinking about my team, and I hope you do, too.

 If you could have anyone you wanted in your team, backing you, who would it be? You can pick someone you admire from outside your life—maybe a famous sportsperson, a musician, or a scientist? You could even choose a fictional character like Spider-Man, or you could make up your own person and decide they are rooting for you. Whoever you've chosen, imagine having a pep talk with them. What would they say to you?

2. LOVE YOUR TEAM!

It's so important to be kind to the people around you. One of my favorite ways to do this is to let people know why I appreciate them and what I am learning from them. Sometimes I can get a bit shy doing this, but I really enjoy it, and I hope they do, too. If you're feeling a little unsure or if you're worried you might struggle to find your words, like I do sometimes, here is a simple game plan you could follow:

- **"I NOTICE THAT . . ."**
  For example, I could say to Kelly, "I notice that you have helped me meet lots of people who are passionate about the same issues I am, and who know how to make a difference."

- **"THIS MAKES ME FEEL . . ."**
  For example, I could then say to Kelly, "This makes me feel really supported and that you really understand what matters to me."

- **"I JUST WANT TO SAY . . ."**
  Then I could finish off by sharing with Kelly, "I just want to say thank you for being you."

YOU DON'T HAVE TO FOLLOW THIS LITTLE GAME
PLAN, YOU MIGHT HAVE YOUR OWN WAY THAT
WORKS FOR YOU. THE IMPORTANT THING IS TO
SAY THANK YOU TO THE PEOPLE YOU ARE GRATEFUL
FOR. YOU MIGHT JUST MAKE THEIR DAY!

7

I KNOW I'VE BROUGHT IT UP A FEW TIMES, BUT I AM REALLY PROUD OF WHERE I COME FROM.

Wythenshawe doesn't have the best reputation, but let me tell you right now, some of the best people I know come from Wythenshawe. It might not be the wealthiest area, or be in the news too much, but there's a **LOT** of talent in Wythenshawe. There are good artists, great street soccer players, and really caring teachers. There are people living there who used to help me when I was a kid; people who are still there now, helping the next generation. And there are children all over Wythenshawe just like me, with big dreams and loads of potential, just looking for the right path to walk down.

THIS WAY

THAT WAY

I learned so many things while growing up in Wythenshawe. You already know how I worked on my soccer skills there, but I also learned how to be street smart and the importance of keeping your head on a swivel (always looking around and taking in new information when you're out and about). Wythenshawe taught me why it's important to be polite to everyone in the community—from the people who run the shops, to the teachers, to the trash collectors—everyone who contributes to the place you live.

I'm really connected to where I come from, and growing up in Wythenshawe I learned how to be curious and ask questions. I learned to question why things were the way they were, and to ask if they could get better. It taught me that when someone says, "You can't do that," I could ask myself, **"Why not?"** This wasn't just so I could learn to be confident in myself, but also because I genuinely wanted to see what was possible.

YOU CAN'T DO THAT.

WHY NOT?

So this is my message to you now—when someone tells you that you can't do something, ask yourself **"Why not?"** and go from there. The support I had as a child helped me to realize that I could chase my dreams with my whole heart, and I want all of you to feel empowered in the same way that I did. You can achieve anything. I really mean that.

Up to this point, I've told you a lot of my story; now I want to show you how to tell yours. We've spoken about the importance of figuring things out on your journey—what you like, how you like to learn, what dreams you have, and how you want to chase them—but you'll also find that you encounter things you care about along the way. Not just for yourself and where you want to go in life, but for the people and places around you. You might get passionate about something, and you might decide to try to change the world because of it.

I'M SERIOUS ABOUT THAT LAST PART, BY THE WAY. YOU REALLY CAN CHANGE THE WORLD AROUND YOU IF YOU'RE PASSIONATE AND WORK HARD. I REALLY WANT YOU TO BELIEVE THAT FOR YOURSELF.

It's great when other people believe in you, but when you believe in yourself? It takes you to a completely different level. That's why when somebody tells me I can't do something because of who I am or where I come from, I can never accept it. I always think, **"Why not? Why can't I?"**

I WANT TO BE REALLY CLEAR, THOUGH: I DON'T WANT YOU TO USE THIS THINKING TO JUSTIFY DOING WHATEVER YOU WANT. I DON'T WANT YOU TO ASK YOURSELF "WHY NOT?" BEFORE DOING SOMETHING DANGEROUS, EITHER FOR YOURSELF OR PEOPLE AROUND YOU. I DO IT, AND THINK ABOUT EACH SITUATION, BECAUSE EVERYTHING IS IMPOSSIBLE UNTIL SOMEONE DOES IT, AND THIS THINKING HELPS ME FIND WAYS TO TURN THE BIG DREAMS INTO REALITIES.

I would love to see a world where children ask themselves **"Why not?"** and realize how much is possible in their lives. Your background does not stop you from achieving amazing things, and growing up with little—no matter what form that might come in—does not mean you're not capable of amazing things. Different people have different experiences, and sometimes the expert on a situation might be the person you'd least expect.

Wythenshawe might not have the best reputation, but growing up there gave me everything I needed to chase my dream to become a soccer player, and then to do even more things away from the game. It's because I didn't grow up with that much that I understood what it was like for children who might be going hungry. I knew what that felt like, and I hope my experiences were useful in getting their voices heard.

DON'T EVER THINK YOUR BACKGROUND IS A REASON WHY YOU CAN'T BE HEARD— NO MATTER WHERE YOU START, DON'T LET THAT DETERMINE WHERE YOU FINISH.

AND WHEN YOU'RE ASKING YOURSELF "WHY NOT?" EVEN WHEN YOUR ANSWER IS "BECAUSE I CAN'T DO IT ALONE" OR "I NEED TO LEARN MORE ABOUT THIS," DON'T THINK OF IT AS THE END OF YOUR JOURNEY THERE AND THEN. There were plenty of things that I wasn't quite able to do when I was a teenager that I'm better equipped to do now as an adult. Sometimes the answer to a "why not?" will make you pause, but it doesn't have to stop you entirely. Your answer can simply be showing you a different route you need to take on your journey. If you care about something, you can come back to it in time, with more skills and a different approach, if needed.

It wasn't until I was 17 that I felt comfortable enough to start talking about some of the things I wanted to change in my area, like making it a bit safer for kids at the park playing soccer, and even then there were other issues I was still figuring out.

As I've gotten older and entered the world of professional sports, I've had to deal with even more complex topics, including racist abuse and other forms of hatred and intolerance. I've told you before that I don't have all the answers, and one thing I'm learning is that sometimes you will never quite know all the answers on a certain topic. I'm not going to pretend that racism doesn't affect me, or that I have the perfect answer for stopping it. I do know that, as a Black man, sometimes I will encounter things designed to try to break my spirit, things that try to make me feel as if I don't belong because of the color of my skin. That is wrong, and I will do whatever I can, for as long as I can, to stop it; not just for myself, but for other people like me, too.

You might encounter complex challenges like this in your life and not be sure of what to do. If that happens, I think it can be helpful to break these challenges up into smaller pieces and try to learn about them as you go along. I started reading a lot more books that were about these harder topics so that I could learn and understand how they affected me and others. From that, I discovered some steps I could take to help and how to try to make sure the next generation don't have it as hard. **GRADUALLY I GOT MORE CONFIDENT TALKING ABOUT THESE ISSUES, AND THEN I BEGAN TO TRY TO MAKE CHANGES.**

There are always going to be people out there who will try to stop you using your voice. They might think that your opinion doesn't count because of your age, the color of your skin, where you come from, or how much money you have—when we were growing up, some people thought Abby couldn't play soccer because she was a girl, and they tried to overlook and dismiss her.

I've never quite understood why someone would want to dismiss people based on how they look, or where they come from. I think it's important to be respectful when you encounter people different from you, and I always try to be someone who listens, learns and asks questions. Especially when I meet someone from another culture, someone who has had different experiences to me or who has a different perspective. Using your voice and standing up for what you believe in is important, but so is being respectful. The way I see it, I have two ears and one mouth, so I should always try to listen more than I talk. Humility is a trait that I get from my mum, and I know that if I went around talking about things I didn't know about, or taking credit for other people's hard work, it wouldn't be right.

I DON'T KNOW THE ANSWERS TO EVERY PROBLEM— SOMETIMES I DON'T EVEN KNOW THE RIGHT QUESTIONS TO ASK!—BUT I KNOW THAT IT'S IMPORTANT TO BE PASSIONATE, TO LISTEN, AND TO TRY TO TAKE IN AND UNDERSTAND WHAT OTHER PEOPLE ARE SAYING.

That leads to the next step: Once you start to hear other peoples' voices, you start realizing that everybody's the same. We all need to eat food, we all need to drink water, and we all need to find a way to get along. We're all human, and we need to look after each other. I've learned that the more you speak to people and the more you listen, the more you learn. Not just people from your neighborhood and environment, but people from all walks of life, people of all ages, shapes, and sizes.

IF YOU LISTEN AND LEARN, AND YOU MIX THE RIGHT PEOPLE TOGETHER, GREAT THINGS CAN HAPPEN.

YOU'RE NOT THE ONLY ONE
RESPONSIBLE FOR CHANGING
THE WORLD, BUT

YOUR VOICE

CAN MAKE A

HUGE

DIFFERENCE.

I can't win a game of soccer on my own, and I couldn't have made this book by myself. The campaigns I have taken part in wouldn't have been as effective if it didn't have help from people up and down the country. **CHANGE CAN BE A GRADUAL PROCESS, AND YOU'LL OFTEN NEED HELP TO GET THINGS DONE. BUT DON'T WORRY, IF YOU WORK HARD FOR SOMETHING, AND YOU WORK WITH THE RIGHT PEOPLE, THEN THE CHANGE <u>WILL</u> COME.**

The food poverty campaign that I am part of has been one of those situations. When we first started on this journey, lots of people were confused about why we were trying to help children who qualified for school meal vouchers over the summer holidays. But, like I said before, I used to be one of those children. The breakfast club I attended and the meals I got given at school were really important to how I grew up, because they helped give my life an extra bit of structure—I knew that no matter what else was going on in my life there was somewhere I could eat, be a kid, and hang out with my friends for just a little bit. So when the pandemic hit and the country first went into lockdown, I realized there were loads of children who might have to go without a meal during their day. I knew it was important that those children who usually went to breakfast clubs and youth groups still had some structure and knew that they would get at least one meal a day, no matter what.

When I first started using my voice to help these children, there were people who said I should "stick to soccer," and others who said that we wouldn't be able to help any children at all. But again I asked, "Why not?" Why wouldn't you see all those people who needed help and then try to do something? What has being a soccer player got to do with trying to help people?

I'LL ADMIT THERE WERE TIMES WHEN I WAS WORRIED ABOUT HOW THINGS WOULD DEVELOP—WHEN YOU'RE TRYING TO MAKE A BIG CHANGE IN THE WORLD AROUND YOU, YOU HOPE THAT YOU ARE DOING THE RIGHT THING AND THAT OTHER PEOPLE CARE ABOUT IT AS MUCH AS YOU DO. AND WHILE THERE HAVE BEEN SOME SETBACKS ALONG THE WAY, AND WE ARE STILL NOWHERE NEAR FINISHED, WHAT WAS IMPORTANT FOR ME IS THAT PEOPLE WHO NEEDED HELP STARTED TO GET THE HELP THEY NEEDED.

That's why I love the environment and the community I grew up in so much; they both showed me the importance of listening, learning, and looking after one another. My plan was always to give back as an adult, but I found that when you start to help one person and hear their story, you'll naturally end up meeting lots more people who you want to help, too. I didn't really think that far ahead when I started using my voice—the plan at first was to help children over the school holidays, but when I found there were other places and communities like Wythenshawe, which had children who were growing up with little, I wanted to do more than just cover the holidays. Together, thanks to the hard work of a lot of people, we can hopefully help those in need for much, much longer.

My mum taught me that when you believe in what you are doing, you don't need to get too bothered by what other people are saying about you. For me, the reward of helping just one family would always outweigh any risk of being criticized. The good work you do will stand for itself.

Right now there are people campaigning against food poverty in a way I couldn't even imagine when we started. I wanted to use my voice for something I believed in, and amazingly that helped other people speak up for what they believed in, too. Now, when we take a step back and see all the incredible things that have happened, it takes my breath away. More and more people are seeing a problem, and rather than thinking, **"That's just the way it is,"** they are saying, **"Why don't we try to change things?"** After we started the campaign, I even had a call from a young boy called Ben who's set up a full marathon to raise money for charity! He was only 10 years old, but he was already using his voice to help people. That sort of thing really excites me. It shows that we live in a world where people see a problem and think "I want to help" rather than walk on by. That's how we make changes in the world.

If you see something that bothers you, remember that you're allowed to say, "This bothers me." If you see a situation where you think you can help, then why not try to help? Your voice can make a difference, and I think you might be surprised by what happens next.

If you're reading this and thinking about using your voice to help others, then why not look into changes you can make in your local area, where you're in a familiar place and know how things work already. Maybe there's a local river or a field that could do with cleaning up, or there might be a way you can get more people outside playing sports. Maybe the change could be to do with food, or you could go around the area fundraising for charity. It doesn't have to be anything big, but if you look into making small changes that can improve the environment around you, I can pretty much guarantee that you'll bump into other people who want to do the same thing. All of a sudden, you could have two, ten, twenty, or one hundred people who are wanting to help out. The first step is often the hardest, but you might surprise yourself with what is possible once you start exploring. Start small and gradually get bigger.

Within you right now is the power and potential to do amazing things.

YOU HAVE A VOICE THAT HAS THE POWER TO CHANGE THE WORLD. HOW YOU USE THAT IS UP TO YOU.

1. FIND YOUR VOICE

When I tell you that you have a voice that has the power to change the world, how does it make you feel? Did you already know that, or was this news to you? Knowing you have a voice is one thing, using it is another, so let's take some time now to think about what you care about.

- **What do you enjoy?**
- **When do you feel like the best version of yourself?**
- **What problems do you see in the world that you'd like to help with?**
- **What opportunities do you see in the world to make a difference? It doesn't matter how big or how small!**
- **What would you like to be involved in?**

Whether you find these questions easy or difficult, the main thing is to try hard to answer them honestly. I don't want you to answer them how you think you should to impress someone else, but how **you** really feel. Finding your voice is a process of discovery. This means that **your** voice is already within **you**—you don't need to make it up, you

just need to discover it. It might help to talk about these questions with a friend or someone in your family. If you answer them really honestly, you'll find your voice, and that is the beginning of great things.

2. DOUBT YOUR DOUBTS

As you know, when someone tells me I can't do something, I like to ask myself, "Why not?" Everything is impossible until someone does it. But what if the person telling you that you can't do it is you? How do you deal with the doubt in your own head? Well, first of all, I want you to know that that feeling is normal. All of us have doubts. Here are some tricks that help me stay true to myself that I hope will help you, too.

- Remember that **thoughts are not facts**. Whenever you try something new—whether it's learning a new skill in school, learning a new instrument or sport, or planning how to use your voice, it's natural to have worries about whether you'll be successful. When you notice worries and doubts popping up, remind yourself this is good news, it means you're stepping out of your comfort zone (and that is where the magic happens). If your thoughts are holding you back, try to break them down and think about where they are coming from: *IS THIS THOUGHT 100% TRUE? WHAT WOULD THINGS BE LIKE IF I DIDN'T BELIEVE THIS THOUGHT? HOW DO I WANT TO THINK INSTEAD?*

Think of your doubts as temporary visitors. You can carry on planning how to use your voice with them in your head. If you're quite creative you might like some of these tricks: see your doubts as leaves on a stream, and watch them float away, or as clouds in the sky. No matter how gray the clouds are, you'll know that above the clouds is blue sky. That blue sky contains the possibilities of your dreams.

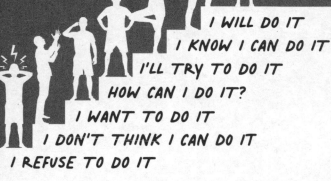

3. BUILD YOUR TEAM!

As you know by now, I have my mum to thank for teaching me the importance of humility. To me, being humble isn't about being quiet or a pushover, but about having confidence in what you do. Do things the way you want to, to the best of your ability, and you'll find you don't need to shout about it from the rooftops; the good work will speak for itself.

There are lots of things that make someone a good team player, but for me, it really boils down to three things:

- **HUMILITY**—A team player cares about the cause and the team more than themselves. They share credit with everyone, they are okay with the fact that they don't know everything, they will talk openly about mistakes, and they know that success is a team effort not down to any one person.
- **HARD WORK**—Team players are willing to work really hard to create change. They will go above and beyond, getting involved in whatever needs doing.
- **CARING**—A team player wants to help people, they listen to others and find the right way to get things done.

Any time we want to do something great, we need to build a team. It might just be you and a friend, or it might be other people in your family, school or even your community. Have you ever heard of Eliud Kipchoge? He is a Kenyan runner. When he set a world record for the marathon, he had 43 pacemakers (people running with him to help him) and many of them were the best runners in the world!

So, now it's time to think about your team:

My Team Member:	I would like their help because:
My mum would probably be first on the list.	She is hardworking and doesn't worry about what other people think.

ONCE YOU'VE MADE YOUR LIST, EVEN IF IT ONLY HAS ONE PERSON ON IT, GO AND ASK FOR THEIR HELP!

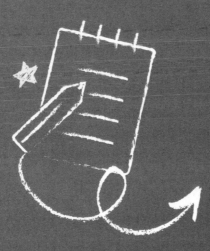

8

THIS IS IT, FRIENDS. THE FINAL CHAPTER.

(YES, I AM CALLING YOU MY FRIENDS NOW. WE'VE SHARED SOME GOOD STORIES TOGETHER, SO I THINK WE CAN BE FRIENDS.)

This is where the book draws to a close, but I want it to be the start of something for you, not the end. Because even though I've tried my best to pass on some lessons about my life so far and what I've picked up along the way, I don't want you to think my learning has stopped. I'm not the finished version of Marcus Rashford, either on or off the field.

Trust me, the learning never stops.

And that's the fun part.

WHEN MOST PEOPLE TALK ABOUT EDUCATION AND LEARNING, THEY TELL YOU ABOUT THEIR SCHOOL DAYS, SO I WANT TO TELL YOU A LITTLE BIT ABOUT MINE. I went to a nursery called Old Moat and stayed there until year two, and then I went to Button Lane Primary School until year six. I was at Sale High for a year of secondary school, and then in year eight, I went to Ashton on Mersey, where I stayed until college. That's a LOT of school, right? Lots of teachers and lots of lessons (and LOTS of homework!), but lots of fun, too.

I loved going to school. I loved seeing my friends every day and playing soccer during break time. I didn't exactly know how all the stuff I was learning in lessons would be useful later in life, but there was something good about going to school in the morning and then coming home in the afternoon just a little bit smarter than you were before.

One of my favorite teachers ever is a woman called Miss Willum, who taught at Button Lane. She did a bit of everything—she ran the breakfast club, helped out with the caretaking, and set up after-school clubs for acting and music—and I still go and visit her whenever I'm around my old primary school. She was still teaching when my nephews went to Button Lane, too, and it's been really cool watching the next generation pick up the same tips she taught me years ago.

Miss Willum showed me that learning was all about exploring—she wanted me to find out what interested me, and then she'd encourage me to discover more about it. I think that's a great way to learn. Even now when I discover a song I like, I'll always look up who made it and then find other musicians who make similar music. For me, learning is all about planting seeds, having those seeds grow into massive trees, and then picking up all the fruit that they drop.

I LOVE LEARNING NOW, BUT WOULD YOU BELIEVE ME IF I TOLD YOU I WASN'T ALWAYS GREAT IN THE CLASSROOM? NINE TIMES OUT OF TEN YOU'D FIND ME SAT IN THE BACK ROW, AND . . . HOW CAN I PUT THIS? I WASN'T THE MOST ATTENTIVE STUDENT.

I was a proper back-seat boy in class, and while I got all my work done, I didn't take my classes seriously until around year nine, which was when I was getting started with Manchester United's academy. That was a turning point for me, and I started to get really passionate about school. Maybe it's because I'm competitive—if you put a test in front of me I'm going to try my hardest to do well. (When I was preparing for my science GCSE, I used to keep on repeating the same things out loud around the house, just to get the facts to stick in my head—I must have driven my family nuts!)

That was my experience. I know I was fortunate that going to school was enjoyable for me and that, in the end, I managed to make lessons fun, too. I know that's not true for everyone. If you're reading this and thinking, *Marcus, I don't like anything about going to school*, then . . . I'm sorry, I wish that wasn't the case. School should be enjoyable for everyone, and there should always be something about it that you find interesting.

Not all of it,

but at least a few things,

at least some of the time.

There were some days when I didn't want to go to school (my mum still made me, though!), but what helped me get through it was trying to see the more difficult parts of school from other people's perspective. Teachers weren't giving me homework because they wanted to stop me from playing soccer or to cut into my weekends; they did it because they wanted to give their students the best chance of being successful.

Friends can also help a lot at school when things are tough. Although there were some kids at school who didn't like me for some reason, which hurt for a bit, I decided to focus on my own friendship group and how to look after that. If I wasn't good at a subject or if I wasn't enjoying it, I would always try to spend time with a friend who was good at it and try to learn from them.

It can be very difficult to concentrate sometimes, or to learn something when you're unhappy, so when you're having a tough time at school, try breaking things up into parts and seeing if you can find something about it that does make you happy. It can be a teacher you like, the after-school club, hanging out with your friends, or even just break time. Sometimes you can almost forget about the work itself and remember that school is a great place to simply be, rather than a place where you need to constantly do tasks. Hopefully, if you get to a place where you feel comfortable at school, then the work will become second nature. You'll find it easier to learn when you're in a happy environment, and you learn better when you can enjoy yourself. Then, when you start to enjoy yourself, you'll find learning is about **patience, perseverance, and possibilities**, just as much as it is about **putting pencil (or pen) to paper.** Don't ever feel that you have to be the person at the front of the class answering all the questions in order to be learning (but if you are sitting at the front answering questions, I want you to know that's great, too!).

YOU CAN LEARN IN WHATEVER WAY IS **RIGHT FOR YOU.**

AND WHEN YOU APPROACH YOUR EDUCATION, IT'S IMPORTANT TO REMEMBER THAT SCHOOL ISN'T THE BEGINNING OR THE END OF IT. SCHOOL IS SO IMPORTANT TO GIVE YOU THE BEST POSSIBLE START IN LIFE, BUT THERE'S SO MUCH OUT THERE IN THE WORLD FOR YOU TO LEARN.

Think of all the things you'd learned before you even set foot in a classroom—like how to talk, how to walk, how to make friends, and so much more! Think of all the things you learn outside of school, too, like your favorite music, what you find funny and what your favorite foods are. You don't stop learning when you're on school holidays— the person you were at the end of year five was just a little bit different compared to the person you were when you started year six. School is an important building block in how you learn, but it's important to keep building on it, constantly.

THOUGH YOU MIGHT NOT ALWAYS FEEL IT, YOU ARE SLOWLY WORKING TOWARD SOMETHING THAT WILL ONE DAY BE INCREDIBLE. EVEN IN YOUR LOWEST MOMENTS. MY COACHES OFTEN SAY

YOU DON'T TAKE LOSSES, YOU TAKE LESSONS

and I always try to keep that in mind if I'm in a bit of a dip. Not just things that help you improve and be productive, but also soft skills, stuff that goes into your personality, even during times when you might not be enjoying yourself. **You're listening, learning, and applying skills every single day.** So I want you to keep your eyes and ears open for new experiences and to try to experiment wherever possible. You've probably done this loads of times already without even noticing.

Do you remember the first time you went to a restaurant with a drink machine? Did you combine two drinks? You know, mixing up the cola and the Fanta until you made something just right? Some might call that cooking, some might call that science, others might not even see that as learning, but I'd say that's using your brain to create something interesting where there wasn't that option before.

Learning is about curiosity and exploration, and part of my passion for education came from looking at the ways I could apply the lessons I was learning in the classroom to the real world. *THE SKILLS YOU PICK UP AT SCHOOL ARE INVALUABLE TO DAY-TO-DAY LIFE—AND I'M NOT JUST TALKING ABOUT DOING SUMS IN YOUR HEAD WHEN YOU'RE AT THE SHOPS.* Up until I was about 14, I used to think that soccer was all I needed to focus on, but at the academy, they showed me how everything Miss Willum and my other teachers had taught me could be applied to all aspects of life—in ways I never could have imagined. When I'm on a soccer field I have to work out angles, like in a math class, and think about momentum when I hit a ball, like in a science class. It's also really important for me to communicate with my teammates effectively, so all that reading out loud in English class comes in use there. (It's also useful for me to be able to communicate in Spanish, and sometimes Italian, too! Learning languages is really fun when you start talking to people from all over the world, in interviews or even as teammates.)

Math and science classes taught me the skills I use to hit free kicks in soccer, but you know where I also picked up lessons? From my family, my friends, and my community. You know that Wythenshawe made me street smart and showed me how to think my way quickly out of problems, and I definitely use lessons I picked up playing soccer on the block when I'm playing at Old Trafford. If I'm up against a defender and he keeps tackling me when I'm trying to dribble past him, I'll have a think and come up with a new plan. I take the street smarts, combine it with the lessons my nanna gave me about having multiple ways to solve a problem, put in some of the school lessons I learned, then layer in all the things soccer coaches have taught me, and voilà! The more you learn, the more you combine different parts of your brain. You become versatile and able to take on anything.

STREET SMARTS

VOILÀ

+

NANNA

COACHES

+

SCHOOL ... +

WE'RE NEARING THE END OF OUR JOURNEY TOGETHER, AND I HOPE YOU'RE FEELING ENERGIZED AND READY TO TAKE ON THE WORLD . . . BUT I WANT TO SPEND JUUUUST A LITTLE BIT MORE TIME TALKING TO YOU ABOUT THE VALUE OF PATIENCE IN YOUR JOURNEY.

I was the most impatient kid you could imagine, but patience is really important to all learning. You will have times when you want things to move faster, but remember this isn't a race against anyone else. It doesn't matter if you learn how to play the guitar at 13 or at 23, or even 73, what matters is you're learning how to do something you enjoy. Patience was an important skill for me to learn, and to be honest, I don't get it right all the time, even now.

You also have to persevere. I like the saying

NOTHING CHANGES, IF NOTHING CHANGES

and I use it a lot in my learning. I can't just say "I want to learn guitar" and then not practice. I have to change my habits to get the changes I want in my life. When you're trying to learn a new skill, it's important you don't stop. Practice is so important. You can take breaks, especially when you're tired, or sick or not feeling 100%, but if you want to learn, it's always good to keep at it.

PERSEVERANCE MEANS YOU'RE ALWAYS KEEPING YOUR POSSIBILITIES OPEN, EVEN IF YOU'RE NOT SURE WHAT THE NEXT STEP IS. YOUR MIND IS AN INCREDIBLE THING: RIGHT NOW THERE ARE SKILLS IN YOU THAT YOU'VE BEEN BUILDING UP SINCE THE DAYS WHEN YOU LEARNED HOW TO WALK AND TALK, AND THEY WILL ALL HELP YOU IN THE YEARS TO COME. So keep developing them, keep honing your skills whenever you can, and you'll be ready to take the next step when the time comes. If you want to get to the top of whatever it is that you're doing, then there are going to be plenty of ups and downs that you need to overcome. So you need to be resilient and persevere when things get tricky.

Now for the possibilities. I hope you have taken something for you from this book, but I hope even more that this is just the start of something for you. This book was an idea I had to help to give you a gentle push to see all the things out there that are worth exploring—I wanted to pass on some of the lessons I've picked up in my life, and I hope they help you figure out something in your life. I believe that my generation is very different from the generation before us and has had to deal with a whole load of different issues, and there's no doubt that's going to be the case for the next generation, too.

THERE ARE
SO MANY DOORS
THAT WILL OPEN
FOR YOU,
SO DON'T WORRY
IF THEY HAVEN'T
ALL UNLOCKED YET.

They will, in time. When you close this book, I want you to start thinking about your journey and how to become a champion in all the things you want to do in life. How to champion other people who may need help, and how to champion causes that you are passionate about. How to champion yourself and believe in yourself. Remember, your dream and your journey belong to you.

Whether you want to be a soccer player, a singer, a teacher, or a veterinarian, or if you want to do something else that barely anyone has even heard of, your dream is YOUR dream, so treat it like that. Go out and chase it with everything you've got, and remember that you are only in competition with yourself.

It won't always be easy, but you will get there.

Now, I've got two final sayings for you that I want to pass on before this book ends. They've both helped me a lot in life:

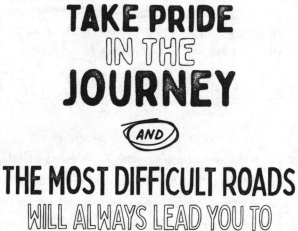

**TAKE PRIDE
IN THE
JOURNEY**
AND
**THE MOST DIFFICULT ROADS
WILL ALWAYS LEAD YOU TO
THE MOST BEAUTIFUL
DESTINATIONS.**

I don't think I'll ever be the final version of Marcus Rashford, because I will never stop learning. I don't ever claim to have the answers to everything, but I think that's the point. I know I'm working hard to get better all the time, and I want you to know that you don't have to be perfect to do the things you want to do in life. It's all part of a process— one of learning, understanding, looking after one another, and, in the end, hopefully one of growth.

I want to say thank you so much for joining me on the journey through this book, and I hope that something you've read here might help you going forward. I want you to know that I believe in you. I really do. I think that you, the person you are as you're reading this now, if you keep your mind open, your heart full, and surround yourself with people that love and appreciate you, then there are no limits on what you can do.

NO LIMITS WHATSOEVER.

NOW GO OUT THERE AND BE A CHAMPION.

M.R.

CHAPTER EIGHT
ACTION POINTS

I'VE GOT ONE MORE TASK FOR YOU. IT'S A LITTLE DIFFERENT FROM THE OTHERS, AND I HOPE YOU ENJOY IT.

When I was younger and beginning to explore a career in soccer, I made a list of things I wanted to do that I would check off one by one—almost like a contract to myself.

I used to keep this list in my head (and sometimes scribbled down in places!) whenever I wanted to remind myself about my life's journey, and why I was walking down my chosen path.

Now I'd like to pass on the practice to you; why don't you have a go doing a contract for yourself? About the journey you want to have, the goals you want to reach, and the people you want to help along the way?

I'm really honored that you've spent a little bit of time on your journey reading about mine, and I'm really excited to see what incredible things you're going to do in yours.

Always remember, there's a bunch of people out there wishing you all the best. And I'm so proud to be part of that team, cheering you on in your journey.

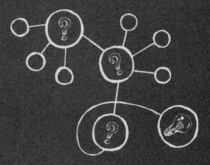

Grab a piece of paper and write out the following:

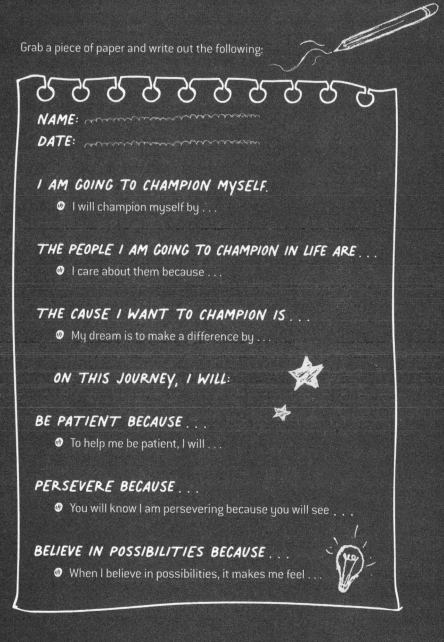

NAME:

DATE:

I AM GOING TO CHAMPION MYSELF.

  - I will champion myself by . . .

THE PEOPLE I AM GOING TO CHAMPION IN LIFE ARE . . .

  - I care about them because . . .

THE CAUSE I WANT TO CHAMPION IS . . .

  - My dream is to make a difference by . . .

ON THIS JOURNEY, I WILL:

BE PATIENT BECAUSE . . .

  - To help me be patient, I will . . .

PERSEVERE BECAUSE . . .

  - You will know I am persevering because you will see . . .

BELIEVE IN POSSIBILITIES BECAUSE . . .

  - When I believe in possibilities, it makes me feel . . .

AFTERWORD

BY TIM S. GROVER

Thank you to my great friend Marcus Rashford for inviting me to contribute to this very important book.

Like all the superstar athletes I have worked with, such as Michael Jordan, Marcus understands that winning isn't about what happens at the end of the match or season. Winning is about what you do EVERY DAY, how you live your life and how you work to get better in all ways. Winning is about committing yourself to being great in everything you do, and being RELENTLESS in your drive toward excellence. Not just in your sport, but also in your schoolwork, your friendships, and your family.

I have three rules for the athletes I work with. ANYONE can do all three of these things, whether you are the best on your team or you are just starting to play. And if you can do them well, they will set you apart from everyone else.

1. SHOW UP

Everything starts with how you show up. Are you focused and prepared? Do you know what you're supposed to do? It's not enough to just be there physically—you must be there mentally as well. The greats show up when they don't feel like it, when they're tired, and when they have other things to do. And when they show up, they are focused and ready to compete and WIN. Showing up means giving your best effort all the time and setting an example for everyone else to follow.

2. WORK HARD

Everyone has the ability to work hard. Even if you are not the most talented player, even if you have a lot to learn, hard work will instantly make you better at anything you do. And if you are already very good, you can always get better. Ask Marcus. He never stops working to improve on his skills and abilities. That's how the best get better, every day. They are never satisfied with their achievements; they always want more for themselves and for their teammates.

3. LISTEN

Pay attention to the coaches, teachers, and parents who want to help you. Hear what they are saying, and understand why it matters. Pay attention to what's happening in your game, during practice, or in the classroom. If you're thinking about what you have to do later, or what happened earlier, or you're distracted by others who don't care about winning, you can't succeed. True champions know they always have more to learn, and they listen to those who can teach them how to be even greater than they already are.

If you can do those three things—**SHOW UP**, **WORK HARD**, and **LISTEN**—you will be well on your way to understanding what it takes to be a champion. Always believe in yourself, strive to be the very best that you can be, and you will already be a champion.

Tim S. Grover has been the trainer, mentor, and adviser to sports' greatest icons, including Michael Jordan, and hundreds of champions in sports and business. He is the bestselling author of RELENTLESS: From Good to Great to Unstoppable *and* WINNING: The Unforgiving Race to Greatness.

ABOUT THE AUTHORS AND CONTRIBUTOR

Marcus Rashford MBE is Manchester United's iconic number 10 and an England International soccer player.

During the lockdown imposed due to the COVID-19 pandemic, Marcus teamed up with the food distribution charity FareShare to cover the free school meal deficit for vulnerable children across the UK, raising in excess of twenty million pounds. Marcus successfully lobbied the British government to U-turn policy around the free food voucher program—a campaign that has been deemed the quickest turnaround of government policy in the history of British politics—so that 1.3 million vulnerable children continued to have access to food supplies while schools were closed during the pandemic.

In response to Marcus's End Child Food Poverty campaign, the British government committed four hundred million pounds to support vulnerable children across the UK, supporting 1.7 million children for the next twelve months.

In October 2020, he was appointed Member of the Order of the British Empire in the Queen's Birthday Honours. Marcus has committed himself to combating child poverty in the UK, and his book, *You Are a*

Champion, is an inspiring guide for children about reaching their full potential.

Carl Anka is a London-born journalist and broadcaster who likes his tea with milk and one sugar. He has written for the BBC, the *Guardian*, *VICE*, *NME*, *GQ*, and BuzzFeed, among other publications online and in print, and specializes in writing about pop culture, video games, films, and soccer. Currently a reporter for sports media group The Athletic covering Manchester United, he is a host of the *Talk of the Devils* podcast and is scared of talking on the phone.

Along with Marcus Rashford, Carl is the cowriter of *You Are a Champion: How to Be the Best You Can Be*—a positive and inspiring guide to life for young readers.

Katie Warriner is one of the UK's leading performance psychologists, working in diverse performance arenas from the sports field to the boardroom, the helicopter pad to the operating room. Her clients include CEOs, Olympic champions, Premiership Rugby teams, and educational leaders. Above all, Katie is passionate about supporting people to be the best they can be and helping them live their lives with purpose.

She has been embedded within Team Great Britain for the last decade, supporting many of the most successful athletes and coaches at the London 2012 and Rio 2016 Olympic Games. She works closely with business leaders to create environments where people can thrive and find meaning in their work. Her belief in potential has also taken her into education, where her work with the charity 21st Century Legacy has helped over 250,000 young people discover their potential. Katie now runs a number of mindset training courses for young people, adults, and aspiring athletes, with the vision of making inspiring and practical mental skills training accessible for all.

Katie lives in Leamington Spa with her husband, Remi, and their daughter, Ayla.